TRUE BLUE BAY
Resort & Villas

Follow the wave to a tropical Caribbean paradise, where aquamarine seas sparkle in the morning sun. Dine on exquisitely crafted Creole cuisine, lounge in comfortable waterfront accommodation, and mingle with our guests and friendly Grenadian staff.

Enjoy a distinctive personal touch developed by the owners Russ, Magdalena and daughters Marie and Renatta Fielden.

Grenada, West Indies
Tel: 473 443 8783
USA: 888 883 2482
mail@truebluebay.com
www.truebluebay.com

Visions of
GRENADA
CARRIACOU & PETITE MARTINIQUE

Introduction

Following the devastation to this beautiful island by Hurricane Ivan in September 2004, closely followed by Hurricane Emily in July 2005, Grenada, along with its sister islands of Carriacou and Petite Martinique, has bounced back with typical resilience. The strength and determination of Grenada's people and natural environment to overcome adversity has prevailed, once again Grenada is back to its picturesque glory.

As a Grenadian living in the UK, I have regularly visited Grenada for business and pleasure over the past 20 years. I have always been in awe of Grenada's breathtaking views and for many years, I contemplated the idea of producing a book to capture this.

Having seen how quickly and easily this picturesque image was taken away by the forces of nature, albeit temporarily, I was inspired to make my vision a reality to celebrate the amazing beauty, character and warmth of this Caribbean jewel and those who call it home.

Visions of Grenada was born.

I believe that words are not enough to capture the magic of this island, so rather than writing about it, I have decided to let Grenada speak for itself through photographic images of its spectacular scenery and culture. The rest is up to you....

Angus Thompson

Contents

THE CARENAGE - THIS PICTURESQUE NATURAL HARBOUR WAS FORMED BY AN ERUPTED VOLCANO CRATER

○ *European settlers careened (put on the side) their ships here, hence the name 'Carenage'*

A VIEW OF PETITE MARTINIQUE FROM CARRIACOU

○ The fruit of the Cacao (Cocoa) tree. The seeds of this fruit are washed, dried and bagged for export, where it is processed into Cocoa Powder, Chocolate and Cocoa Butter. Grenada's Cocoa is considered to be of the highest quality.

○ *FORT FREDERICK*

○ FINANCIAL COMPLEX - ST. GEORGES

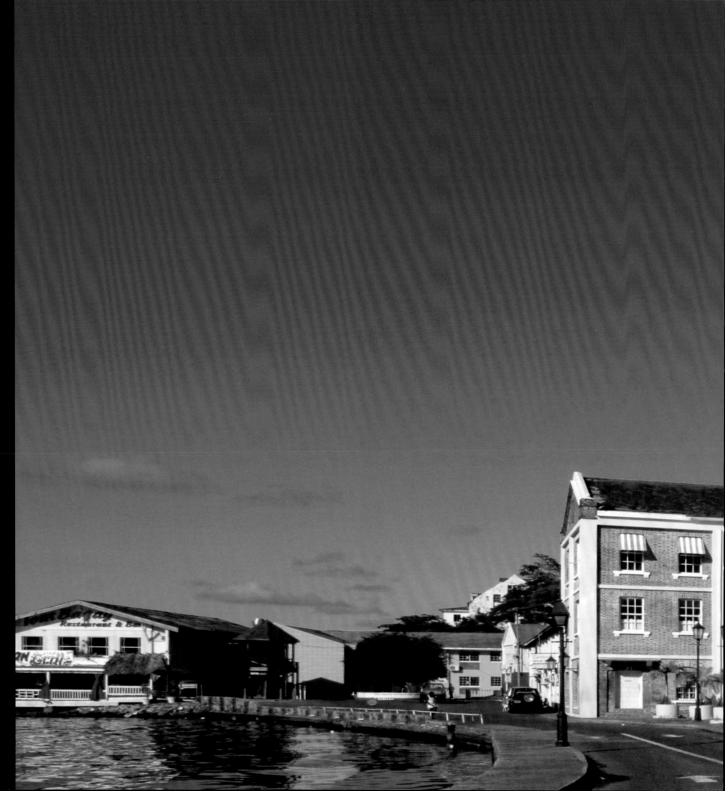

○ **NUTMEG - GRENADA'S MOST VERSATILE AND IMPORTANT SPICE**

● *THE INNER NUT IS USED FOR FLAVOURING SAVOURY AND SWEET DISHES*

● *THE RED MEMBRANE IS DRIED AND GROUND INTO SPICE MACE*

● *THE OUTER YELLOW LAYER IS USED TO MAKE JAMS, JELLIES AND SYRUPS*

● *THE HARD SHELL AROUND THE INNER NUT IS USED BY LOCALS FOR FLOWERBED MULCH*

● *THE NUTMEG IS ALSO USED FOR MEDICINAL PURPOSES TO RELIEVE JOINT AND MUSCLE PAIN*

O *THE LUSH VEGETATION OF CARRIACOU*

The vibrant colours of Carnival...

○ THE COLOUR AND FUN OF GRENADA'S CARNIVAL IS ONE OF THE HIGHLIGHTS OF THE YEAR

Beach life...

La Sagesse beach - St. Davids

○ CORAL COVE BEACH

○ LOWER SECTION OF MARQUIS FALLS

A lavish landscape of lush greens and waterfalls...

○ CONCORD FALLS

WINDMILL RUINS
PROTECTED SITE

○ MARQUIS FALLS - ALSO KNOWN AS MOUNT CARMEL FALLS, THE HIGHEST WATERFALL IN GRENADA

○ KNOWN AS MOUNT CARMEL FALLS, THE HIGHEST

BBC Beach

Into the big blue.....

THE COLOUR AND SPECTACLE OF WORLD-CLASS RACING YACHTS IN COMPETITION

○ *GRENADA OFFERS PERFECT SAILING FOR LOCAL COMPETITION AND INTERNATIONAL EVENTS*

○ *DRAMATIC SKY, BEAUTIFUL OCEAN*

For the love of Sport...

○ GRENADA'S NEW CRICKET STADIUM, BUILT IN TIME FOR HOSTING STAGES OF THE WORLD CUP CRICKET TOUR 2007

ICC Cricket World Cup 2007

○ THE VIRGIN HOLIDAYS GRENADA CRICKET CLASSIC WAS DEVISED BY THE GRENADA BOARD OF TOURISM TO DEVELOP ITS SPORTS-TOURISM POTENTIAL. MANAGED AND TAILAORED THROUGH GRENADA SPORTS, WHICH WAS OPERATED BY THE FORMER ENGLAND CRICKETER ALLAN LAMB AND NIGEL FELTON.

THEY WERE SUCCESSFUL IN ATTRACTING THE IDEAL SPONSORS TO CONCUR IN BRINGING TO GRENADA SOME OF THE TOP FORMER PLAYERS FROM ENGLAND AND THE WEST INDIES TO REVITALISE THE RIVALRY OF THE FORMER GLORY DAYS OF TEST MATCH CRICKET BETWEEN THE TWO NATIONS.

IN THE FIRST YEAR OF COMPETITION, THE ORIGINAL GRENADA NATIONAL STADIUM WAS THE VENUE FOR THE TWO-MATCH ONE-DAY SERIES. IN THAT INSTANCE EACH TEAM WON A GAME. HURRICANE IVAN IN 2004 CAUSED THE COMPETITION TO BE MOVED TO THE RURAL PARISH OF ST. ANDREW IN 2005. AT THE SAME VENUE IN 2006 THE WEST INDIES WON BOTH RURAL GAMES.

CRICKET IS NOT THE ONLY SPORT PLAYED WITH ENTHUSIASM ON THE ISLAND

JASON ROBERTS - GRENADA'S INTERNATIONAL FOOTBALLER, JASON ROBERTS WAS BORN 25 JANUARY 1978 AND STARTED OUT AS A TRAINEE AT CHELSEA FC. JASON HAS PLAYED FOR WEST BROMWICH ALBION, WIGAN ATHLETIC AND IS CURRENTLY WITH BLACKBURN ROVERS FC PLAYING IN THE ENGLISH PREMIER LEAGUE. JASON IS PROUD TO HAVE REPRESENTED GRENADA IN INTERNATIONAL FOOTBALL AND IS ONE OF TWO FULL TIME PROFESSIONAL PLAYERS IN THE SQUAD. IN 2007, JASON LAUNCHED HIS OWN CHARITY "THE JASON ROBERTS FOUNDATION" TO PROVIDE A RANGE OF SPORTING OPPORTUNITIES FOR CHILDREN AND YOUNG PEOPLE IN THE UK AND GRENADA

○ WORLD-CLASS PLAYER DEVON SMITH

DEVON SMITH - BORN ON 21ST OCTOBER 1981 IN ST. PATRICK, GRENADA, DEVON SMITH IS A LEFT HAND BATSMAN IN THE WEST INDIES CRICKET TEAM. THE GRENADIAN OPENER HAS MADE VALUABLE CONTRIBUTIONS TO THE WI TEAM AGAINST INTERNATIONAL OPPOSITION; SCORING 91 AGAINST THE TOURING INDIANS A YEAR AGO AND LATER THAT SEASON, BEING THE LEADING RUN-SCORER ON THE WEST INDIES A TOUR IN ENGLAND, WITH HIS AGGREGATE OF 465, INCLUDING 181 AGAINST LANCASHIRE. HE HAS ALSO ENJOYED TWO PRIME FIRST-CLASS CAMPAIGNS, LEADING THE WINDWARD ISLANDS' BATTING WITH 572 RUNS IN 14 INNINGS.

Grenadan Sportsmen on the world stage...

LEWIS HAMILTON *IS THE FIRST PERSON OF AFRO-CARIBBEAN DECENT TO COMPETE IN FORMULA ONE (F1) GRAND PRIX. BORN ON 7TH JANUARY 1985, THE GRANDSON OF A GRENADIAN WHO MIGRATED TO BRITAIN IN THE 1950s, LEWIS BEGAN RACING GO-KARTS AT AGE 8, HE PROGRESSED TO CAR RACING AND SUBSEQUENTLY BECOME THE YOUNGEST EVER DRIVER TO SECURE A F1 CONTRACT AT THE AGE OF 13 YEARS.*

LEWIS MADE HIS IMPRESSIVE DEBUT IN F1 RACING FOR THE MCLAREN-MERCEDES TEAM ON 18TH MARCH 2007, WHERE HE PLACED 3RD IN THE AUSTRALIAN GRAND PRIX. HE SUBSEQUENTLY PLACED 2ND IN THE MALAYSIAN, BAHRAIN, SPANISH AND MONACO GRAND PRIX RACES AND 1ST IN THE CANADIAN AND US GRAND PRIX RACES, PRESENTLY LEADING THE CHAMPIONSHIP TABLE. THIS MAKES HIM THE YOUNGEST DRIVER EVER TO LEAD THE F1 DRIVERS' CHAMPIONSHIP, AND THE ONLY DRIVER TO EVER FINISH IN THE TOP THREE IN ALL OF HIS FIRST SEVEN GRAND PRIX RACES.

THOUGH STILL EARLY IN THE CHAMPIONSHIP, LEWIS HAS MADE AN INCREDIBLE ENTRANCE TO F1 RACING AND HAS THE POTENTIAL TO BECOME THE GREATEST RACING DRIVER IN F1 HISTORY.

○ *LEWIS WITH HIS GREATEST SUPPORTER - FATHER ANTHONY*

○ *LEWIS'S TALENT WAS SPOTTED VERY EARLY IN HIS CAREER BY MCLAREN F1 SUPREMO RON DENNIS*

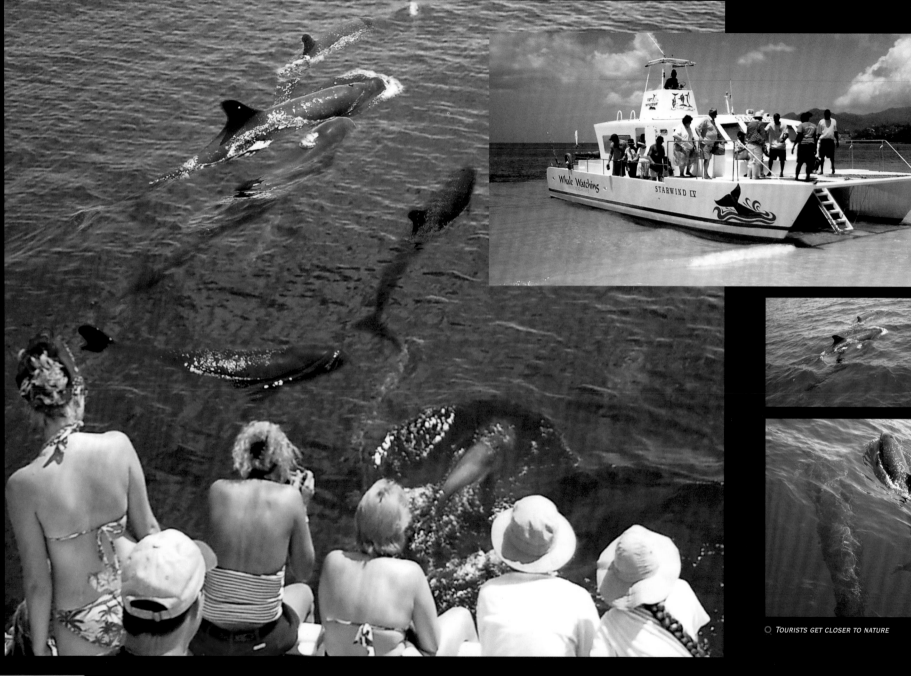

○ TOURISTS GET CLOSER TO NATURE

○ *Enjoying beach life is a regular pastime for all the family in Grenada*

○ *SNORKELING IN THE CRYSTAL-CLEAR WATERS*

TOMORROW'S WORRY

Relaxing retreats...

○ CALABASH HOTEL

○ WORLD-RENOWNED CHEF GARY
RHODES AT THE CALABASH HOTEL

THE HOTEL'S 'RHODES RESTAURANT'
IS GARY RHODES' ONLY RESTAURANT
OUTSIDE THE UK

○ *TRUE BLUE BAY RESORT*

© BANA VILLAS

○ La Sagesse Nature Centre

○ Green Roof Inn on Carriacou

○ Grenada Crowne Plaza Resort

○ *The Spice Island Beach Resort*

○ REX GRENADA RESORT

○ *Grand View*

○ BELAIR PLANTATION VILLA RESORT

○ *CORAL COVE*

FLAMBOYANT HOTEL

142

BARRY COUNTRY RETREAT

WAVE CREST HOLIDAY APARTMENTS

ALLAMDA BEACH RESORT

○ SOUTH CITY PLAZA HOTEL

LA SOURCE

BELAIR GARDEN COTTAGE IN CARRIACOU

JENNY'S PLACE

○ CINNAMON BEACH CLUB

○ BOGLES ROUND HOUSE & COTTAGES

○ Coyaba Hotel Pool

A garden of Eden...

○ *Suzanne Gaywood*

Short History Of Grenada At Chelsea

Having an exhibit for Grenada in the Great Pavilion at Chelsea was an ambition fulfilled in 1998 by Floral Designer Suzanne Gaywood & her small, dedicated team of helpers.

The exhibits have been awarded medals in each of the last 9 years, with five consecutive gold's, 2001 – 2005, and now the Grenada team has won gold again in 2007, their 10th year.

Made up of the major growers & plantsmen of Grenada along with the design team based in the UK, the Grenada At Chelsea Team face the challenges each year of exhibiting at the world's most prestigious flower show, and the opportunity of showcasing the beautiful island through its exotic flora.

○ MARKET VENDORS ARE GENERALLY BRIGHTLY-DRESSED RURAL WOMEN WHO CREATE A LIVELIHOOD FOR THEMSELVES BY SELLING SPICES AND A WIDE VARIETY OF LOCAL PRODUCE IN THE ST. GEORGE'S MARKET.

THIS NEWLY REFURBISHED ESTABLISHMENT HAS A HISTORY OF THESE FRIENDLY AND COLOURFUL INDIVIDUALS WHO ENJOY THEMSELVES PURSUADING LOCALS AND VISITORS TO PURCHASE THEIR MERCHANDISE.

IN SOME INSTANCES THEY'RE WIVES OF HARD WORKING FARMERS OR LADIES WHO SEARCH THEIR VILLAGES TO PURCHASE CROPS FROM BONA FIDE FARMERS. IT'S A MUST SEE FOR THE VISITOR WHO TAKES PRIDE IN ABSORBING THE CHARACTER AND LIFESTYLES OF THESE WOMEN. A FEW MEN ALSO VEND STRAW AND LEATHER ITEMS, AS WELL AS COCONUT WATER AND OTHER CRAFT ITEMS.

PAPPY'S PRODUCTS - THIS ONE ROOM BUILDING HOUSES A WIDE ASSORTMENT OF LIQUORS, PAPPY'S MOST POPULAR DRINK IS 'BOIS BANDE' AN APHRODISIAC MADE FROM THE BARK OF A TREE.

Tropical Flavours...

BEAUTIFUL GARDENS AND A WONDERFUL VIEW GREET YOU AT THE WATER'S EDGE RESTAURANT AND BAR

○ DINER'S DELIGHTS...A HIGH STANDARD OF CUISINE BOTH INTERNATIONAL AND LOCAL CAN BE ENJOYED ON THE ISLAND

○ THE FRESHEST INGREDIENTS - PREPARED WITH FLAIR

○ THE AQUARIUM BEACHSIDE RESTAURANT

○ Dodgy Dock Restaurant

○ True Blue Restaurant

Every friday night, the hamlet of Gouyave welcomes locals and visitors to experience the Gouyave Fish Friday. From 6.00 pm to 1.00 am. St Francis and St. Dominic streets are transformed into a seafood extravaganza with freshly-caught fish, shrimp and lobster and other seafoods cooked on open fires in a variety of ways. Participants are allowed to explore the delights found within the many tents. Delights that include local fishcakes, shrimp kebabs, jerked marlin, barbequed snapper and lobster in garlic sauce, washed down with local juices and beverages.

Usually, by 8.00 pm, the entertainment would be in full swing. This incorporates cultural performances that range from steel band music, drummers and DJ's.

The fish Friday Festival encourages community development in a traditional fishing village by promoting it as the fishing capital of Grenada. It forges links with agriculture, craft, tourism and the cultural arts while giving added value opportunities to the St. John's Parish.

The festival is managed by the Gouyave Fish Friday Festival Company - a non-profit making company with representatives from the Fisherman's Association, the Gouyave Improvement Committee, the St. John's Social & Cultural Organization and Gouyave Sailing Club.

Dr. Groom

An island of medical excellence...

○ *PALATIAL GROUNDS AND STUNNING VIEWS GREET STUDENTS AT THE MEDICAL UNIVERSITY*

○ *St George's University* - *Founded 30 years ago initially as a School of Medicine, St George's University now also includes a School of Veterinary Medicine and School of Arts and Sciences with an internationally focused MBA program. To date, over 6,400 doctors and 300 other SGU graduates have adopted the University's philosophy of global education and applied their expertise worldwide.*

Reef life...

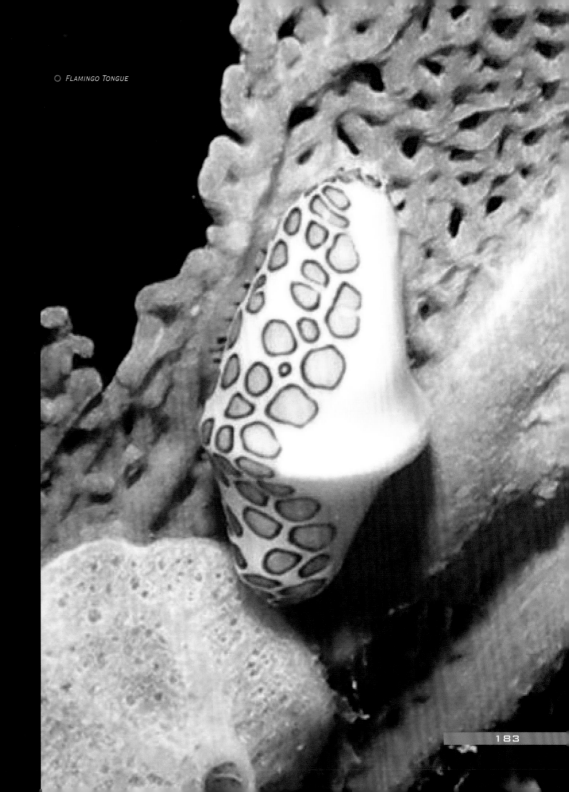

Flamingo Tongue

Divers enjoy observing a large Baracuda

○ *A Moray eel awaits his next snack*

○ Big Eye

○ Wreck diving is a popular sport for visitors and locals

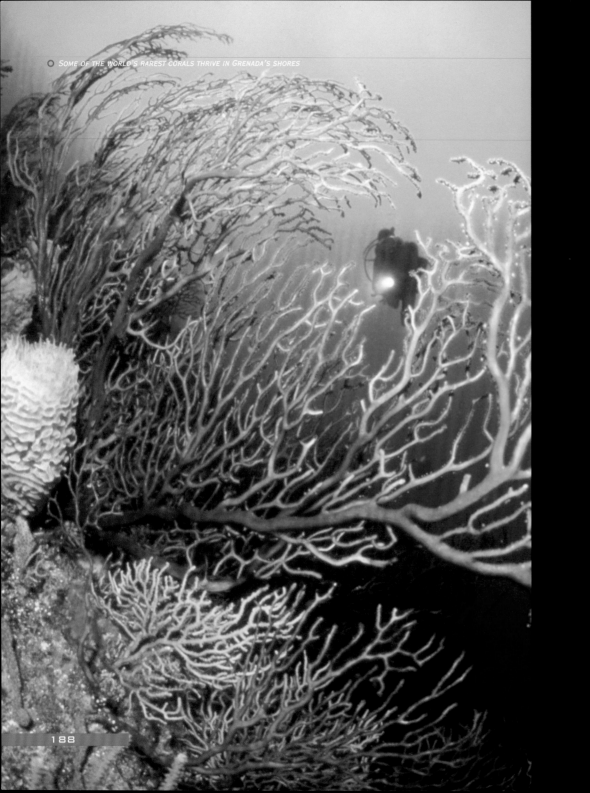

○ SOME OF THE WORLD'S RAREST CORALS THRIVE IN GRENADA'S SHORES

○ AN IMPRESSIVELY ADORNED SEA SLUG

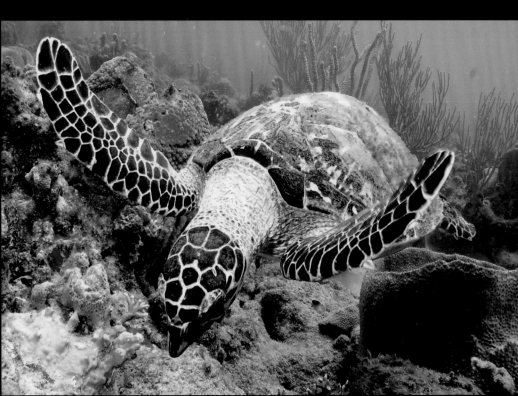

○ SAN JUAN - STERN OF THE 'SAN JUAN' FISHING VESSEL WRECK, WHICH SANK IN 1975

○ BIANCA C - ON ITS FINAL VOYAGE FROM ITALY IN 1961, THIS 600FT CRUISE LINER CAUGHT FIRE AFTER AN EXPLOSION IN THE BOILER ROOM AND SANK, WHILE ANCHORED OFF THE COAST OF ST GEORGE'S. KNOWN AS THE 'TITANIC OF THE CARIBBEAN' THE BIANCA C WRECK IS ONE OF THE MOST EXCITING DIVE SITES IN THE CARIBBEAN, WHICH DIVE EXPERTS HAVE INCLUDED AS ONE OF THE TOP TEN WRECK DIVE SITES IN THE WORLD.

○ THE BRIDGE SECTION OF THE 'SAN JUAN' FISHING BOAT SHIPWRECK IS EXPLORED

Spectacular Sunsets...

About Grenada

CARRIACOU & PETITE MARTINIQUE

"Welcome to Grenada, the Spice of the Caribbean"

JOCELYN SYLVESTER-GAIRY
DIRECTOR OF TOURISM

IT IS STATED THAT ST. GEORGE'S, OUR CAPITAL IS THE MOST PICTURESQUE CITY THIS SIDE OF CAPRI.....THAT OUR PEOPLE ARE THE FRIENDLIEST AND OUR BEACHES ARE UNCROWDED AND PRISTINE.....THAT ONE CAPTURES THE AROMA OF THE SPICES FROM WAY OUT AT SEA.....THAT THE GRENADA EXPERIENCE IS LIKE A VISIT TO MOTHER NATURE'S HOME ON HER VERY BEST DAY.

COME! ENJOY OUR EXOTIC DISHES, DASHING SCENERY, GREAT DIVE SITES, RICH CULTURAL HERITAGE AND LUSH TROPICAL FORESTS.

WELCOME FROM THE GRENADA BOARD OF TOURISM

JOCELYN SYLVESTER-GAIRY - *DIRECTOR OF TOURISM*

NJKOYAN ROBERTS
CHAIRMAN OF BOARD OF TOURISM

PRIME MINISTER DR. THE RT. HON KEITH MITCHELL

KEITH CLAUDIUS MITCHELL, THE SON OF THE LATE DOWLYN AND CATHERINE MITCHELL, WAS BORN AT HAPPY HILL IN THE PARISH OF ST. GEORGE ON NOVEMBER 12, 1946. HE RECEIVED HIS PRIMARY EDUCATION FROM THE HAPPY HILL ROMAN CATHOLIC SCHOOL AND THE J.W. FLETCHER MEMORIAL SCHOOL. HIS SECONDARY EDUCATION WAS UNDERTAKEN AT THE PRESENTATION BROTHERS COLLEGE.

DR. MITCHELL STUDIED AT THE UNIVERSITY OF THE WEST INDIES, CAVE HILL CAMPUS, WHERE HE GAINED A BACHELOR OF SCIENCE DEGREE IN MATHEMATICS AND CHEMISTRY (1969-71), FOLLOWED BY A MASTERS DEGREE IN MATHEMATICS FROM HOWARD UNIVERSITY (1973-75) AND A DOCTORATE IN MATHEMATICS AND STATISTICS FROM THE AMERICAN UNIVERSITY (1975-79).

DR. MITCHELL SERVED AS A TEACHER AT THE PRESENTATION BROTHERS COLLEGE FROM 1972-73 AND AS A MATHEMATICS PROFESSOR AT HOWARD UNIVERSITY FROM 1977-83. HE WORKED AS A PROFESSIONAL CONSULTANT TO SEVERAL GOVERNMENT DEPARTMENTS AND PRIVATE CORPORATIONS IN THE UNITED STATES OF AMERICA, BEFORE RETURNING TO HIS HOMELAND GRENADA.

IN 1984 DR. MITCHELL WAS ELECTED TO THE HOUSE OF REPRESENTATIVES AS THE MEMBER OF PARLIAMENT OF ST. GEORGE'S NORTH WEST. HE IS THE LONGEST SERVING MEMBER IN THE HOUSE OF REPRESENTATIVES. HE SERVED AS MINISTER OF COMMUNICATIONS, WORKS AND PUBLIC UTILITIES, TRANSPORTATION, CIVIL AVIATION AND ENERGY FROM 1984 TO 1988 AND MINISTER OF COMMUNICATIONS, WORKS AND PUBLIC UTILITIES, COOPERATIVES, COMMUNITY DEVELOPMENT, WOMEN'S AFFAIRS AND CIVIL AVIATION FROM 1988 TO 1989 IN THE NEW

NATIONAL PARTY (NNP) GOVERNMENT. HE CONTINUED AS AN OPPOSITION MEMBER OF PARLIAMENT UNTIL 1995.

DR. MITCHELL WAS ELECTED POLITICAL LEADER OF THE NNP IN 1989. HE SUCCESSFULLY LED THE NNP TO VICTORY IN THE 1995 GENERAL ELECTION AND BECAME PRIME MINISTER ON JUNE 22, 1995.

FROM 1995 TO 1999 DR. MITCHELL SERVED AS PRIME MINISTER, MINISTER OF NATIONAL SECURITY, MOBILISATION, CARRIACOU AND PETITE MARTINIQUE AFFAIRS, FINANCE, TRADE, INDUSTRY AND PLANNING, INFORMATION AND FOREIGN AFFAIRS. HE CURRENTLY HOLDS THE PORTFOLIOS OF MINISTER OF FINANCE, NATIONAL SECURITY AND INFORMATION.

In the 1999 election, Dr. Mitchell led the NNP to an unprecedented victory, winning all 15 constituencies and being the first Prime Minister since Independence to win two consecutive general elections.

Dr. Mitchell led the NNP to another unprecedented victory on November 27, 2003, when the Party was elected to a third consecutive term in Office. The Prime Minister holds the portfolios of National Security, Human Resource Development, Information, Information Communication Technology (ICT), Business and Private Sector Development and Youth Development.

In the field of sports, Dr. Mitchell has contributed significantly in the area of cricket. He was a member of the Grenada Cricket Team from 1964-66, captain of the Combined Windward and Leeward Youth Cricket Team in 1966 and the Grenada Cricket Team in 1973.

The Prime Minister continues to play cricket. He initiated the informal Prime Ministerial Cricket Series in 2000, in an effort to promote the sport and contribute to the process of Regional Integration. Prime Minister Mitchell also supports many sporting events through personal sponsorships.

In his capacity as Prime Minister, Dr. Mitchell has served as Chairman of the Caribbean Community (CARICOM) from January to July 1998 and from July to December 2004; Chairman of the Board of Governors of the Caribbean Development Bank from May 1997 to May 1998; Chairman of the Ministerial Council of the Association of Caribbean States from 1996 to 1997.

Prime Minister Mitchell has been responsible for Science and Technology and Human Resource Development for CARICOM since July 1995.

Prime Minister Mitchell is Chairman of the CARICOM Prime Ministerial Sub-committee on Cricket.

Prime Minister Mitchell served as Chairman of the Organisation of Eastern Caribbean States (OECS) from May 2000 to January 2002, being the longest serving Chairman of the regional sub-group.

Prime Minister Mitchell served as Chairman of the Regional Security System (RSS) from April 2001 to March 2002.

The Prime Minister was appointed by Her Majesty to the Privy Council on February 20, 2004. As a result, his title is: Dr. the Right Honourable Keith Mitchell, PC, MP. He and his wife Marietta have one son, Olinga.

Office Address: **Office of the Prime Minister, Sixth Floor, Ministerial Complex, Botanical Gardens, St. George's, Grenada; tel:** 1-473-440-2255/2265/2383; **fax:** 1-473-440-4116; **email:** HYPERLINK "mailto:pmoffice@gov.gd" pmoffice@gov.gd

Grand Etang Crater Lake

General Information

MODERN GRENADA

GRENADA IS A DEMOCRATIC COUNTRY AND AN INDEPENDENT NATION WITHIN THE BRITISH COMMONWEALTH. THE STATE OF GRENADA INCLUDES CARRIACOU AND PETITE MARTINIQUE. THE HEAD OF STATE IS HER MAJESTY, THE QUEEN, WHO IS REPRESENTED LOCALLY BY A GOVERNOR GENERAL. THE COUNTRY IS GOVERNED BY A 13-MEMBER SENATE AND A HOUSE OF REPRESENTATIVES, WITH A SPEAKER AND 15 MEMBERS, EACH REPRESENTING A CONSTITUENCY. PRIME MINISTER KEITH MITCHELL IS SERVING HIS THIRD TERM IN OFFICE.

HURRICANE IVAN STRUCK GRENADA IN SEPTEMBER 2004 CAUSING SEVERE DAMAGE, FROM WHICH THE ISLAND IS MAKING A REMARKABLE RECOVERY.

SOCIAL CONVENTIONS

LOCAL CULTURE REFLECTS THE ISLAND'S HISTORY OF BRITISH AND FRENCH COLONIAL RULE AND, OF COURSE, THE IMPORTED CULTURES OF ENSLAVED AFRICANS. AFRICAN INFLUENCE IS ESPECIALLY NOTICEABLE ON THE ISLAND OF CARRIACOU IN THE BIG DRUM AND IN GRENADA IN THE SHANGO DANCE. THE ROMAN CATHOLIC CHURCH ALSO EXERTS A STRONG INFLUENCE ON THE WAY OF LIFE.

NEW YEAR HONOURS, 2007

SEVEN GRENADIANS WERE AMONG THOSE HONOURED IN THE QUEEN'S 2007 NEW YEAR'S HONOURS:

- **GORDON STEELE, OBE,** *CONTRIBUTION TO BANKING*
- **LAWRENCE LAMBERT, CBE,** *CONTRIBUTION TO TOURISM*
- **CYNTHIA CRUICKSHANK, MBE,** *CONTRIBUTIONS TO PUBLIC SERVICE*
- **JEAN ROBINSON, MBE,** *OUTSTANDING SERVICE IN COMMUNITY DEVELOPMENT*
- **HORATIO BRIZAN, MBE,** *CONTRIBUTION TO BUSINESS*
- **NORRIS MARSHALL, BEM,** *FOR FARMING*
- **ANTHONY GEORGE, BEM,** *FOR ART AND CULTURE*

○ SUPERLINER DOCKS AT THE NEW PORT COMPLEX - ST. GEORGES

MILITARY HONOURS, 2005

IN MARCH 2005, PRIVATE JOHNSON GIDEON BEHARRY, WAS AWARDED THE VICTORIA CROSS (VC), BRITAIN'S HIGHEST MILITARY HONOUR, FOR ACTS OF EXCEPTIONAL BRAVERY DURING THE IRAQI WAR. PRIVATE BEHARRY WAS BORN IN DIEGO PIERCE, ST MARK'S IN 1979, AND LEFT SCHOOL AT 13. IN 1999 HE JOINED THE PRINCESS OF WALES'S ROYAL REGIMENT, SUBSEQUENTLY SERVING IN KOSOVO, NORTHERN IRELAND AND IRAQ. IN MAY 2004, WHILST ON DUTY IN IRAQ, HE WAS COMMENDED FOR HIS 'VALOUR OF THE HIGHEST ORDER', FOR ASSISTING AMBUSHED FOOT PATROLS. A MONTH LATER, DESPITE SUFFERING SEVERE HEAD INJURY, WHEN HIS VEHICLE WAS HIT BY A ROCKET-PROPELLED GRENADE, HE DROVE TO SAFETY SAVING HIS INJURED COMMANDING OFFICER AND CREW, BEFORE COLLAPSING. HE WAS AWARDED THE VC WHILE RECOVERING FROM BRAIN SURGERY. YOU CAN READ HIS REMARKABLE STORY IN: BAREFOOT SOLDIER, BY JOHNSON BEHARRY AND NICK COOK, PUBLISHED 2006.

BRIEF HISTORY

GRENADA HAS HAD A TURBULENT HISTORY. SOME TIME BEFORE AD1300, THE ARAWAKS, THE ISLAND'S EARLIEST KNOWN INHABITANTS, WERE DISPLACED BY THE CARIBS, WHO WERE STILL IN OCCUPATION WHEN CHRISTOPHER COLUMBUS VISITED GRENADA IN 1498. A BRITISH ATTEMPT TO SETTLE IN 1609 WAS FIERCELY RESISTED BY THE CARIBS AND IT WAS NOT UNTIL 1650 THAT THE FRENCH WERE ABLE TO CLAIM THE ISLAND. DURING THE NEXT 200 YEARS THEY ESTABLISHED SUGAR ESTATES IMPORTING LARGE NUMBERS OF ENSLAVED AFRICANS TO WORK THEM. THE BRITISH CAPTURED GRENADA FROM THE FRENCH IN 18TH CENTURY AND EXPANDED SUGAR PRODUCTION. THE ENSUING POWER STRUGGLE BETWEEN THE FRENCH AND BRITISH CONTINUED UNTIL 1783, EVENTUALLY SETTLED BY THE TREATY OF VERSAILLES WHICH GAVE GRENADA, CARRIACOU & PETITE MARTINIQUE TO THE BRITISH.

THERE WAS AN UNSUCCESSFUL ATTEMPT IN 1795 BY JULIEN FEDON, A FRENCH-AFRICAN PLANTER AND OTHER 'FREE COLOUREDS' AND SLAVES TO OVERTHROW THE BRITISH. HOWEVER, SLAVERY WAS NOT ABOLISHED IN GRENADA UNTIL 1838. IN THE EARLY 20TH CENTURY GRENADIANS, LED BY T. A. MARRYSHOW, BEGAN TO CHALLENGE THE BRITISH CROWN AND PLANTERS. THEY SUCCEEDED IN SETTING UP TRADE UNIONS IN THE 1930'S, BUT DID NOT HAVE THE WORKING CLASSES SUPPORT.

○ LANCE CORPORAL JOHNSON BEHARRY VC

IN FEBRUARY 1974 ERIC GAIRY, A FORMER TEACHER, MOBILISED WORKERS AND LED GRENADA TO INDEPENDENCE FROM THE UK, MAKING GRENADA ONE OF THE SMALLEST INDEPENDENT COUNTRIES IN THE WESTERN HEMISPHERE. FIVE YEARS LATER GAIRY WAS DEPOSED IN A BLOODLESS COUP BY THE NEW JEWEL MOVEMENT (JOINT ENDEAVOUR FOR WELFARE, EDUCATION AND LIBERATION), MADE UP OF MAINLY YOUNG, EDUCATED LEFT-WINGERS LED BY MAURICE BISHOP. BISHOP WAS KILLED IN A MILITARY COUP IN 1983, GIVING THE USA THE EXCUSE IT NEEDED TO INVADE THE ISLAND TO RESTORE A PRE-NJM SYSTEM OF GOVERNMENT. THE NEW NATIONAL PARTY (NNP), FORMED UNDER THE LEADERSHIP OF THE VETERAN POLITICIAN HERBERT BLAIZE, WON THE GENERAL ELECTION IN DECEMBER 1984, AND HAS DOMINATED GRENADIAN POLITICS EVER SINCE.

ECONOMY

GRENADA IS KNOWN AS 'SPICE ISLAND' AND UP TO THE 20TH CENTURY, SPICE WAS ITS BIGGEST EARNER OF FOREIGN CURRENCY. TODAY, TOURISM HAS REPLACED NUTMEG AS THE MAIN SOURCE OF FOREIGN EXCHANGE, WITH THOUSANDS OF PEOPLE ARRIVING EACH YEAR BY AIR AND SEA.

POLITICAL MOVERS AND SHAPERS

THEOPHILUS ALBERT MARRYSHOW (1887-1958) — 'FATHER OF THE FEDERATION', IS A PIVOTAL FIGURE IN THE POLITICAL HISTORY OF GRENADA AND THE CARIBBEAN. MARICHEAU TO GIVE HIM HIS BIRTH NAME BEGAN AS A RADICAL REFORMER BUT ENDED AS THE ELECTED REPRESENTATIVE FOR ST GEORGE'S. HIS FIRST JOB IN 1903 WAS DELIVERING NEWSPAPERS FOR W.G. DONOVAN, A PUBLISHER OF RADICAL NEWSPAPERS ADVOCATING REPRESENTATIVE GOVERNMENT AND FEDERATION OF BRITISH WEST INDIAN COLONIES. BY 1915, MARRYSHOW, WHO BY NOW HAD ANGLICISED HIS NAME, WAS A FULLY-FLEDGED JOURNALIST WITH HIS OWN NEWSPAPER, THE WEST INDIAN. IN 1918 HE SET UP THE REPRESENTATIVE GOVERNMENT ASSOCIATION WHICH LED TO CHANGES IN THE WAY MEMBERS WERE ELECTED TO THE LEGISLATIVE COUNCIL IN 1920'S. MARRYSHOW CONTINUED TO BE ACTIVE IN ATTEMPTS TO SET UP A WEST INDIAN FEDERATION AND WAS AT THE ONE AND ONLY MEETING OF THE STANDING CONFERENCE IN 1929 IN BARBADOS.

IN 1931 HE LOBBIED THE COLONIAL OFFICE FOR A MORE REPRESENTATIVE GOVERNMENT IN GRENADA. IN 1937, HE HELPED ORGANISE A NON-VIOLENT DEMONSTRATION IN GRENADA TO SHOW SOLIDARITY WITH STRIKING WORKERS IN OTHER WEST INDIAN ISLANDS. HE RETAINED HIS SEAT IN GRENADA'S FIRST GENERAL ELECTION IN 1951, WHEN GAIRY'S PARTY WON SIX OF THE EIGHT SEATS, AND SAW THE FEDERATION SIGNED INTO LAW IN 1956. HE DIED SHORTLY AFTER BEING NOMINATED TO THE UPPER HOUSE OF THE FEDERAL PARLIAMENT.

○ Rex Beach

SIR ERIC MATTHEW GAIRY (1922 -1997)

Grenada's first and longest serving Prime Minister, defined Grenada's politics for almost a half century. Gairy was a visionary who appointed the first female Governor in the British Commonwealth. He was one of Grenada's representatives at the historic Federation conference in Jamaica in 1957 and one of the founding fathers of Carifta and Caricom. He was handsome, charismatic, controversial and autocratic, and his excesses led to his government being overthrown in 1979. Gairy was born in St. Andrew's and achieved high academic results. He taught at his old school before migrating to Aruba in 1943, returning to Grenada in 1948. In Aruba he became involved in trade unionism through working for the Lago Oil Company. Back home he applied this experience to fight for better working conditions. In the 1950's he achieved what Marryshow could not, mobilising and organising the working classes into effective trade unions. He formed the GMMIWU trade union and Grenada United Labour Party. In 1974 he led Grenada to Independence. In government the 'Land for the landless' was implemented, Grenada was the first Caribbean Island to host an exposition 'Expo69' and also to win Miss World (1970), with Jennifer Hosten. He successfully brought the St. George's University School of Medicine to Grenada.

Bacolet Bay

Bacolet Bay 5-Star Caribbean Living

Paradise Island Living with outstanding potential for capital growth, strong rental yields and the fastest growing tourism market in the Caribbean

- 5-star resort set in 41 acres of tropical gardens
- Full resort management delivering high yields
- Secluded bay with a 200m white-sand beach
- Breathtaking sea views
- Private infinity plunge pools
- On-site luxury hotel, spa, fitness & sports centre
- Direct flights from London, 15 minutes from airport

UK: +44 1865 202 700
Ireland: +353 1 612 1448
USA: +1 646 216 8079
info@propertyfrontiers.com
www.bacoletbay.com

Altman Real Estate (Grenada) Ltd
Tel: +1 473 435 2081
Email: aaa-gda@spiceisle.com

Property frontiers

HERBERT AUGUSTUS BLAIZE (1918-1989) - FIRST CHIEF MINISTER, WAS BORN ON CARRIACOU. HE BEGAN HIS WORKING LIFE AS A SOLDIER, ENTERING POLITICS IN 1957 AFTER COMPLETING A LAW CORRESPONDENCE COURSE. IN 1960 HE WAS APPOINTED CHIEF MINISTER. HE WAS DEFEATED BY GAIRY'S UNITED LABOUR PARTY IN 1961, ONLY TO BE REAPPOINTED CHIEF MINISTER BY THE BRITISH GOVERNMENT A YEAR LATER AFTER THEY REMOVED GAIRY FOLLOWING ACCUSATION OF CORRUPTION. IN 1967 BRITAIN GRANTED GRENADA INTERNAL SELF GOVERNMENT (STATE HOOD) UNDER BLAIZE, BUT, LATER THAT YEAR GAIRY AGAIN DEFEATED HIM. IN 1976 BLAIZE'S GRENADA NATIONAL PARTY JOINED FORCES WITH THE NEW JEWEL MOVEMENT (NJM) IN A FUTILE ATTEMPT TO DEFEAT GAIRY. IN 1979 BLAIZE 'RETIRED' TO CARRIACOU FOLLOWING THE NJM SUCCESSFUL COUP THAT OVERTHREW GAIRY. AFTER THE INVASION OF GRENADA IN 1983, THE AMERICAN GOVERNMENT CREATED THE NEW NATIONAL PARTY (NNP) AND INSTALLED BLAIZE AS PRIME MINISTER. HE SOON LOST CONTROL OF THE NNP AND FORMED A NEW PARTY, TNP. CAUGHT IN AN INDUSTRIAL STRUGGLE WITH THE TEACHER'S UNION AND PUBLIC WORKER'S UNION OVER SALARY, BLAIZE SOLD THE GRENADA TELEPHONE COMPANY FOR LESS THAN ITS VALUE.

MAURICE BISHOP (1944-1983) — WAS BORN ON ARUBA RETURNING TO GRENADA AGE SIX. HE WAS ACADEMICALLY GIFTED WINNING ONE OF THE FEW ISLAND SCHOLARSHIPS. IN 1963 HE LEFT GRENADA TO STUDY LAW AT THE UNIVERSITY OF LONDON. AFTER GRADUATING HE WORKED AS A CIVIL SERVANT. IN 1969 HE WAS CALLED TO THE BAR AND RETURNED TO GRENADA A YEAR LATER. IN 1973 HE FORMED M.A.P (MOVEMENT FOR ASSEMBLIES OF THE PEOPLE) WHICH MERGED WITH UNISON WHITEMAN'S JOINT ACTION FOR EDUCATION WELFARE AND LIBERATION (JEWEL), TO FORM THE NEW JEWEL MOVEMENT (NJM). IN 1976, HE WAS

ELECTED TO THE HOUSE OF REPRESENTATIVES AND BECAME LEADER OF THE OPPOSITION, A POST HE HELD UNTIL 1979. HIS PEOPLE'S REVOLUTIONARY GOVERNMENT (PRG) MADE GREAT ACHIEVEMENTS IN EDUCATION, MEDICAL SERVICES, WORKERS RIGHTS, WOMEN'S RIGHTS, CO-OPERATIVES, POLITICAL AWARENESS, LAND DEVELOPMENT, INFRASTRUCTURE AND STARTED THE INTERNATIONAL AIRPORT. ON 14TH OCTOBER 1983, BISHOP WAS PLACED UNDER HOUSE ARREST. HE WAS RESCUED BY THE PEOPLE AND TAKEN TO THE ARMY'S HEADQUARTERS ON FORT RUPERT. BISHOP WAS EXECUTED ON 19TH OCTOBER BY THE PEOPLE'S REVOLUTIONARY ARMY (PRA).

○ *Sugar Loaf Island off Levera Beach*

Sir Royston Oliver Hopkin, K.C.M.G

Sir Royston Oliver Hopkin, K.C.M.G., has had a distinguished career in the hospitality and tourism industry spanning 41 years. He began his tourism career when he joined the family business at Ross Point Inn in 1965. At 20, he was appointed to the Grenada Tourist Board and elected President of the Grenada Hotel Association at age 24.

In 1969, he was appointed to the Board of Directors of Spice Island Inn, and by 1975 was appointed Deputy Chairman and Deputy Managing Director of the resort. Since 1970, Hopkin served on the Board of the Caribbean Hotel Association (CHA) as Director, Vice President, President and Chairman

In 1978, Hopkin along with brothers Arnold and Gerald, purchased the Blue Horizons Hotel, and in 1986 it was renamed the Blue Horizons Cottage Hotel. In 1989 he became the owner, chairman and managing director of Spice Island Inn, which he renamed Spice Island Beach Resort.

In 2000, the resort underwent a US$6 million transformation and reopened as the "New" Spice Island Beach Resort. In 2004, Hurricane Ivan devastated the resort, undeterred, Sir Royston embarked on a US$12 million dollar project to re-design and renovate the resort, which re-opened on December 15, 2005. The resort now employs 150 staff.

Hopkin received the coveted Caribbean Hotel Association's "Hotelier of the Year" honour in 1991, and Grenada's Silver Anniversary Independence Award for 25 years of dedicated service. In 1995, the Caribbean Tourism Organization honoured Hopkin for more than 25 years of untiring service to Caribbean Tourism. In 2002, he received further awards at their Golden Anniversary Awards Ceremony at the Waldorf Astoria Hotel in New York.

received further awards at their Golden Anniversary Awards Ceremony at the Waldorf Astoria Hotel in New York.

Sir Royston was to establish a Scholarship Fund for needy children, when he adopted the Grand Anse R.C. School in 1992. Every year he gives secondary education scholarships to needy students at the school. Between 1996 and 1997, Hopkin worked in collaboration with the Grenada Union of Teachers and the Ministry of Education, to enlighten teachers about the Tourism Industry and to create a lobby for tourism to be included in the schools' curricula.

In 1994, Queen Elizabeth II bestowed on him the "Companion of the most distinguished order of St Michael and St George" (CMG) for his contributions to Grenada and Caribbean tourism. In the 2004 New Years Honours List, Queen Elizabeth elevated his rank to Knight Commander of the most distinguished order of St Michael and St George (KCMG).

Sir Royston is currently Chairman of the Caribbean Alliance for Sustainable Tourism (CAST), and is a member of the Executive Committee and Honorary Member of the Caribbean Hotel Association. Honorary Director of the Grenada Hotel Association, and Vice Chairman of the Board of Trustees of the Queen Elizabeth Home for Children, a Member of the Grenada Airlift Committee, and a Director of ICC Cricket World Cup WI 2007.

Presently he holds Directorships in: Blue Horizons Garden Resort, Ross Point Inn Ltd., Oliver's Investment Ltd., and George F. Huggins Grenada Ltd.

Hopkin is married to Betty - The Lady Hopkin, and has three children - Ryan, Nerissa and Janelle.

Lord David Pitt (1913 – 1994)

Lord Pitt of Hampstead, was a widely respected political campaigner and leading civil rights activist for equality for Britain's black and minority ethnic communities, as well as being active within the medical profession — being the first ever general practitioner to become President of the British Medical Association.

Lord Pitt of Hampstead in London was born David Thomas Pitt in Grenada in 1913. At age 20 he went to Britain to study medicine at Edinburgh University.

A political activist since his student days, David Pitt became a stalwart in Trinidad and Tobago, where as a practicing doctor, he founded the West Indian National Party in the support of West Indian self-government.

In 1947 David Pitt returned to London to practice medicine and become politically active within Britain's Labour Party, that he first joined in 1936.

As a general practitioner and a political activist, David Pitt came to know and make friends with many of the leading figures in Pan-Africanism and the freedom movements of Africa and Caribbean. He stood unsuccessfully for Parliament on two occasions, however, his many positive achievements include serving as the first black person to become the Chairman of the former Greater London Council (GLC), the President of the British Medical Association (BMA), Deputy Lieutenant of Greater London. Leader of the Campaign Against Racial Discrimination (CARD). At the helm of the Commission for Racial Equality (1968-77).

Leading members of Britain's Caribbean community spearheaded the formation of the charitable Lord Pitt Foundation on the occasion of his 70th birthday. Lord David Pitt was granted a life peerage in 1975 and died 18th December, 1994.

PRICKLY BAY - LANCE AUX EPINES

THE RIGHT-HONOURABLE BARONESS HOWELLS OF ST. DAVIDS, OBE

ROSALIND PATRICIA-ANNE WAS BORN ON THE ISLAND OF GRENADA IN THE WEST INDIES. SHE CAME TO BRITAIN IN 1951 WHERE HER GOOD NATURE DREW MANY TO HER.

IN 1955 SHE BECAME THE FIRST BLACK PERSON TO WORK IN A PUBLIC LIBRARY WHERE SHE MET AND MARRIED JOHN CHARLES HOWELLS AND HAD TWO DAUGHTERS ANNE AND AMANDA.

HER AMBITION TO BECOME A LAWYER WAS PUT ON HOLD. FINANCES WERE LIMITED AND ROS (AS SHE WAS FONDLY KNOWN) TURNED HER HAND TO MANY JOBS TO MAKE ENDS MEET.

HER UPBRINGING IN A POLITICAL FAMILY LEFT HER WITH A RESILIENCE AND SELF BELIEF THAT SHE HAS MARSHALLED IN MANY A STRUGGLE FOR THE RIGHTS OF CARIBBEAN PEOPLE. SHE CONTRIBUTED, IN HER OWN WAY, USING HER SKILL AS A TRAINED WELFARE AND COUNSELLING STUDENT TO PERSUADE OTHERS THEY WERE WRONG IN THEIR ATTITUDE TO THOSE WHOSE SKIN COLOUR, MORE THAN ANY LACK OF SKILL, PREVENTED THEM FROM CONTRIBUTING EQUALLY IN THE WORK FORCE.

IT WAS A FORTUITOUS MEETING WITH A COMMUNITY WORKER IN LEWISHAM THAT GAVE HER THE BREAK SHE WAS LOOKING FOR. ROS ACCEPTED A POST IN THE YOUTH CLUB RUN BY SYBIL PHOENIX TO WORK WITH UNSUPPORTED MOTHERS - IT WAS HERE SHE LEARNT THE TRUE MEANING OF RACISM - PREJUDICE PLUS POWER.

NOT ONLY WAS SHE EXPOSED TO REAL PREJUDICE BUT SHE MET WITH WORKERS WHO WERE DEDICATED TO ERADICATING THE CANCER OF RACISM.

HER SOFT SPOKEN AND WELL THOUGHT OUT ARGUMENTS SOON BROUGHT HER TO THE NOTICE OF

SHE HAD A GENUINE INTEREST IN PEOPLE AND WAS ABLE TO GIVE SPEECHES WHICH HAD A HIGH IMPACT ON PEOPLE, AND MOVED MINDS, NOT ALWAYS VERY WELCOME, BUT ROS HAD THE QUALITY WHICH ALLOWED HER TO MAKE ALLOWANCES FOR THOSE WHO WERE RELUCTANT TO HEED HER WORDS..

SHE WAS CAUGHT UP IN THE LEWISHAM 'SUS' CAMPAIGN AND THE NEW CROSS FIRE. HER APPROACH WAS TO VISIT AND TEND THE VICTIMS RATHER THAN EXPRESS OPINIONS.

ROS MOVED FROM LEWISHAM TO GREENWICH RACE EQUALITY COUNCIL. HERE SHE CAME TO HER OWN - SHE CONFRONTED THE CHURCHES, THE LOCAL AUTHORITY, BUSINESS PEOPLE, AND MANY OTHERS BUT SHE STILL FOUND TIME TO COMFORT VICTIMS' FAMILIES LIKE THE ADAMS FAMILY AFTER ROLAND'S MURDER AND THE STEPHEN LAWRENCE FAMILY - HER HEART AND HOME WERE AT THEIR DISPOSAL.

Ros was invited to sit on many committees - the London Voluntary Service Committee, the Board of the University of Greenwich, the Family Forum, the Training Board of the GLC, the Greater London Race Equality Council, the Year of the Child, Lewisham Racial Equality Council and many more too numerous to mention.

Ros never aspired to become a local councillor or MP but joined a political party because she felt they were more open to 'equal opportunity'.

For her work she was awarded the OBE, yet it was quite a surprise when she was invited to enter the House of Lords. But with her usual grace she accepted the invitation and has served in that capacity since 1999. In all of this Ros has never forgotten her island home - she served for a short time as Deputy High Commissioner pre the revolution. In her words she serves Grenada during its good and its bad times - you will see Ros name as member, advisor and patron of many Grenadian organisations.

A London newspaper says of her: Walking with Lords but she keeps her feet firmly on the ground".

She is often listed among the great and inspirational Britons in London. She takes a keen interest in Caribbean affairs and more recently the African Diaspora.

There are videos like 'Mixed Race Family', 'The Enemy Within', and the New Cross Fire documentaries which laid bear her deep feelings and willingness to help.

His Excellency Joslyn Whiteman

His Excellency Joslyn Whiteman Grenada Ambassador to the People's Republic of China. Former Grenada High Commissioner to the Court of St. James. Former member of the House of Parliament and Minister of Government 1995-2003 Top branch Manager American Life UK. Voted businessman of the year in 1977 by the UK Afro Caribbean Chamber of Commerce for his managerial and outstanding sales performance.

ESPLANADE MALL - ST. GEORGES

Useful Information

POPULATION: 102,632 (EST. JULY 2006)

CAPITAL: ST GEORGE'S

CLIMATE: TROPICAL. THE DRY SEASON RUNS FROM JANUARY TO MAY AND RAINY SEASON FROM JUNE TO DECEMBER. THE AVERAGE TEMPERATURE IS 28C (82°F).

SUGGESTED CLOTHING: TROPICAL LIGHTWEIGHTS AND COOL SUMMER CLOTHING. DRESS IS CASUAL AND INFORMAL BUT MINISKIRTS AND BEACHWEAR IS NOT WELCOME IN TOWN.

TIME ZONE: ATLANTIC STANDARD TIME. GMT- 4. EST +1.

CURRENCY: EAST CARIBBEAN DOLLAR (EC$) = 100 CENTS. NOTES = EC$100, 50, 20, 10 AND 5. COINS = EC$1, 50, 25, 10, 5, 2 AND 1 CENTS.

ELECTRICITY: 220/240 VOLTS AC, 50HZ. MOST HOTELS PROVIDE DUAL VOLTAGE SHAVER UNITS, BUT AN ADAPTER PLUG IS NECESSARY FOR OTHER APPLIANCES.

LANGUAGE: ENGLISH.

RELIGION: ROMAN CATHOLIC 64 %, ANGLICAN 22%, PLUS OTHER SMALLER PROTESTANT DENOMINATIONS.

TIPPING: MOST HOTELS AND RESTAURANTS ADD A 10% SERVICE CHARGE. IF NO CHARGE IS ADDED, IT IS CUSTOMARY TO LEAVE A 10% TIP.

TELEPHONE: FULL IDD SERVICE. COUNTRY CODE: 1473. THERE ARE NO AREA CODES. COIN AND TELEPHONE CARD PAYPHONES ARE WIDELY AVAILABLE. CARDS AVAILABLE FROM CABLE & WIRELESS GRENADA AND OTHER AGENTS.

MOBILE: A GSM 900/1900 NETWORK PROVIDES GOOD COVERAGE FOR MOST OF GRENADA, CARRIACOU AND PETITE MARTINIQUE AND SURROUNDING WATERS. NETWORK PROVIDERS INCLUDE CABLE & WIRELESS CARIBBEAN CELLULAR, TRANS-WORLD TELECOM CARIBBEAN, DIGICEL GRENADA AND GRENADA WIRELESS HOLDINGS LTD. HANDSETS CAN BE HIRED LOCALLY.

FAX: MANY HOTELS ALSO OFFER FAX SERVICES.

INTERNET: INTERNET IS WIDELY AVAILABLE IN GRENADA. SPICEISLE IS THE MAIN ISP PROVIDER.

TELEGRAPH: CABLE & WIRELESS GRENADA OFFER TELEGRAPHIC SERVICES.

CURRENCY EXCHANGE: FIRST CARIBBEAN INTERNATIONAL BANK, RBTT BANK GRENADA LIMITED, GRENADA CO-OPERATIVE BANK, REPUBLIC BANK (GRENADA) LTD AND SCOTIA BANK ARE ALL FOUND ON THE ISLAND.

○ MODERN BANKING FACILITIES

BANKING HOURS: MON-THURS 0800-1400, FRI 0800-1600.

CREDIT/DEBIT CARDS: AMERICAN EXPRESS, DINERS CLUB, MASTERCARD, VISA AND OTHER MAJOR CARDS ARE ACCEPTED BY MOST SHOPS, CAR HIRE COMPANIES AND HOTELS.

TRAVELLER'S CHEQUES: WIDELY ACCEPTED BUT TAKE US$ CHEQUES TO AVOID ADDITIONAL EXCHANGE RATE CHARGES.

CURRENCY RESTRICTIONS: NONE.

POST: THE MAIN GENERAL POST OFFICE IS ON BURN'S POINT, IN ST GEORGES. THERE ARE SUB-POST OFFICES IN ALL TOWNS AND VILLAGES. POSTAL HOURS ARE USUALLY MON-THURS 0800-1530, FRI 0800-1630 (CLOSED WEEKENDS). THE GENERAL POST OFFICE HAS AN EXPRESS MAIL SERVICE, WHICH IS ENHANCED BY INTERNATIONAL COURIERS – FEDERAL EXPRESS, DHL AND UPS.

NEWSPAPERS: SEVERAL NEWSPAPERS, ALL IN ENGLISH, INCLUDING SPICE ISLE REVIEW, GRENADA ADVOCATE, GRENADA TODAY AND THE GRENADIAN VOICE.

RADIO: TEN LOCAL RADIO STATIONS FOUND AT (AM 535 KHZ; AM 1400 KHZ / FM90 KHZ / FM96.3 KHZ; FM 101.7 KHZ; FM105.5 KHZ). BBC WORLD SERVICE AND VOICE OF AMERICA CAN BE RECEIVED, BUT FREQUENCIES OCCASIONALLY CHANGE. CHECK THEIR WEBSITES.

TELEVISION: THERE ARE THREE TELEVISION STATIONS. MANY HOTELS HAVE SATELLITE/CABLE TELEVISION

FOOD/DRINK: MAINS TAP WATER IS CHLORINATED AND SAFE TO DRINK. BOTTLED WATER IS READILY AVAILABLE. MILK IS PASTEURISED, DAIRY PRODUCTS, SEAFOOD, FRUIT AND VEGETABLES ARE GENERALLY CONSIDERED SAFE.

HEALTH: A YELLOW FEVER VACCINATION CERTIFICATE IS REQUIRED FROM ALL TRAVELLERS OVER ONE YEAR OF AGE COMING FROM INFECTED AREAS. IMMUNISATION AGAINST HEPATITIS A, B AND DIPHTHERIA IS SOMETIMES RECOMMENDED. RABIES IS PRESENT. FOR THOSE AT HIGH RISK, CONSIDER VACCINATION BEFORE ARRIVAL. IF YOU ARE BITTEN, SEEK MEDICAL ADVICE WITHOUT DELAY. THERE IS A GENERAL HOSPITAL IN ST GEORGES AND SMALL HOSPITALS IN MIRABEAU AND CARRIACOU. CLINICS AND DOCTORS CAN BE FOUND THROUGHOUT THE ISLANDS. HEALTH INSURANCE IS ADVISED.

ANIMALS: IMPORTATION OF ANIMALS IS PROHIBITED WITHOUT AN IMPORT PERMIT. PROPER HEALTH DOCUMENTS MUST BE PRODUCED AND THE GOVERNMENT VETERINARY OFFICER MUST BE NOTIFIED OF THE PORT OF ENTRY AND THE EXPECTED TIME OF ARRIVAL.

BUSINESS AND COMMERCIAL: ALL CORRESPONDENCE AND TRADE LITERATURE IS IN ENGLISH. OFFICE HOURS: MON-FRI 0800-1200 AND 1300-1600.

CONFERENCES/CONVENTIONS: EIGHT HOTELS OFFER MEETING FACILITIES, SEATING FROM 25 TO 300 PERSONS.

ARRIVING AND DEPARTING GRENADA

BY AIR: GRENADA INTERNATIONAL AIRPORT (POINT SALINES) (GND) IS 11KM (8 MILES) SOUTH OF ST GEORGE'S. FACILITIES INCLUDE DUTY-FREE SHOPS, BUREAU DE CHANGE, CAR HIRE, HANDICRAFT SHOPS, SNACK BARS, BOUTIQUES AND TOURIST INFORMATION.

PASSPORT: ALL VISITORS MUST HAVE A RETURN ONWARD TICKET AND A VALID PASSPORT. FROM JANUARY 23, 2007, ALL U.S. CITIZENS TRAVELING BY AIR TO AND FROM GRENADA MUST HAVE A VALID PASSPORT TO ENTER OR RE-ENTER THE UNITED STATES.

VISA: A VISA IS REQUIRED BY ALL VISITORS EXCEPT CITIZENS OF THE US, CANADA, UK, BRITISH COMMONWEALTH, CARIBBEAN COUNTRIES (EXCEPT CUBA), MOST EUROPEAN COUNTRIES, SOUTH KOREA, AND JAPAN. VISITORS MAY BE REQUIRED TO DEPOSIT AN AMOUNT EQUAL TO THE FARE OF THEIR RETURN PASSAGE.

DUTY-FREE: ALLOWANCE PER PERSON: 200 CIGARETTES OR 50 CIGARS OR 225G OF TOBACCO, ONE BOTTLE WINE OR SPIRITS AND A 'REASONABLE' AMOUNT OF PERFUME.

PROHIBITED: NARCOTICS: ARMS AND AMMUNITION; FRUIT AND VEGETABLES.

AIRLINES FROM THE UK:

BRITISH AIRWAYS, VIRGIN AND GOLDEN CARIBBEAN HAVE WEEKLY DIRECT FLIGHTS FROM LONDON'S GATWICK AIRPORT. BWIA HAS DAILY DIRECT FLIGHTS FROM LONDON'S HEATHROW AIRPORT TO ANTIGUA, BARBADOS, ST. LUCIA AND TRINIDAD, WITH SAME DAY CONNECTIONS VIA LIAT.

FROM CANADA & USA:

AIR JAMAICA HAS DIRECT FLIGHTS FROM NEW YORK / MONTEGO BAY. AMERICAN EAGLE HAS DIRECT FLIGHTS FROM AND TO PUERTO RICO. BWIA OPERATES REGULARLY SCHEDULED FLIGHTS VIA ITS TRINIDAD HUB. AIR CANADA VACATIONS OPERATES A WEEKLY SERVICE FROM TORONTO TO GRENADA DURING THE WINTER SEASON (DECEMBER TO APRIL) WITH EASY CONNECTIONS FROM HALIFAX, MONTREAL AND OTTAWA. AIR CANADA AND BWIA OPERATE REGULARLY SCHEDULED FLIGHTS FROM TORONTO AND MONTREAL TO BARBADOS AND TRINIDAD, WITH CONNECTIONS INTO GRENADA VIA LIAT.

INTER-CARIBBEAN:

LIAT PROVIDE CONNECTIONS INTO GRENADA FROM VARIOUS CARIBBEAN ISLANDS ALONG WITH CONNECTIONS TO INTERNATIONAL FLIGHTS FROM ANTIGUA, BARBADOS, ST. LUCIA AND TRINIDAD. CONVIASA AIRLINES PROVIDES A TWICE-WEEKLY SERVICE FROM PORLAMAR, MARGARITA INTO GRENADA. SVG AIR PROVIDES DAILY FLIGHTS FROM CARRIACOU'S LAURISTON AIRPORT TO GRENADA AND ST. VINCENT.

DEPARTURE TAX: EC$50 PER ADULT, PAYABLE IN CASH. EC$25 FOR CHILDREN FIVE TO 12 YEARS OF AGE. CHILDREN UNDER FIVE ARE EXEMPT.

ARRIVAL BY SEA: GRENADA IS A PORT OF CALL FOR MANY CRUISE LINES, INCLUDING COSTA, CUNARD, PRINCESS, NORWEGIAN CRUISES AND ROYAL VIKING. GEEST LINE SAILS FROM THE UK VIA MARTINIQUE, ANTIGUA, ST LUCIA AND BARBADOS. AROUND 70 PER CENT OF TOURIST ARRIVALS ARE CRUISE-SHIP PASSENGERS. A DAILY SHUTTLE BOAT SERVICE OPERATES BETWEEN GRENADA AND CARRIACOU, AND AN INTER-ISLAND FERRY SERVICE SAILS TO CARRIACOU, PETIT MARTINIQUE AND ISLE DE RONDE FOUR TIMES WEEKLY. HOTELS AND LOCAL TOURIST OFFICE CAN SUPPLY DETAILS OF SAILING TIMES AND FARES.

ENTRY AND DEPARTURE TAXES: VISITORS ENTERING GRENADA BY SEA ARE REQUIRED TO PAY CRUISE (VISITOR) LEVY OF US$3.00 PER PERSON. THE FOLLOWING FEES ALSO APPLY:-

CRUISE PERMIT: (YACHTS)
LESS THAN 40FT EC$ 50.00
40 –60 FT   EC$75.00
60-80 FT   EC$100.00
OVER 80 FT   EC$150.00

SEAPORT DEPARTURE FEES: VISITORS ARRIVING BY AIR AND LEAVING BY SEA, ARE REQUIRED TO PAY AN EMBARKATION TAX OF EC $1.00 PER PERSON, TO THE IMMIGRATION OFFICE AT THE TIME OF DEPARTURE.

WHEN YOU ARRIVE IN GRENADA

GETTING AROUND: ROAD TRAFFIC DRIVES ON THE LEFT. MOST OF THE MAIN ROADS ARE IN GOOD CONDITION BUT THEY CAN BE NARROW AND WINDING. YOU NEED A LOCAL DRIVING PERMIT, WHICH YOU CAN GET FROM MOST CAR RENTAL AGENCIES OR BY APPLYING TO THE TRAFFIC DEPARTMENT AT THE CENTRAL POLICE STATION ON THE CARENAGE. YOU MUST SHOW A BONA FIDE DRIVER'S LICENSE. THE COST IS EC$30.00.

BUSES: THERE ARE BUS SERVICES AROUND THE COASTAL ROADS TO ST GEORGES, THEY ARE CHEAP AND INTERESTING, BUT CAN BE SLOW AND CROWDED. IN CARRIACOU THE MAIN BUS TERMINAL IS LOCATED AT THE WEST END OF GRANBY STREET. MINIBUSES RUN BETWEEN HILLSBOROUGH, WINDWARD AND TYRELL BAY.

TAXI: TAXIS ARE THE MOST EFFICIENT MEANS OF TRANSPORT. THEY ARE AVAILABLE AT THE AIRPORT, THE CARENAGE AND OUTSIDE MOST HOTELS. THERE ARE NO FIXED PRICES SO IT IS IMPORTANT TO ESTABLISH THE FARE WITH THE DRIVER IN ADVANCE. TAXIS CAN BE HIRED FOR ANY PERIOD FOR SIGHTSEEING TOURS.

BICYCLE: BICYCLES CAN BE HIRED — BUT REMEMBER THAT THE ISLAND IS MOUNTAINOUS, TROPICAL AND OUTSIDE THE CAPITAL, ROAD SURFACES CAN BE UNPREDICTABLE.

Useful Information

WATER TAXI: WATER-TAXIS ARE AVAILABLE FROM ST GEORGES ACROSS THE CARENAGE TO THE ESPLANADE OR GRAND ANSE BEACH. CARRIACOU CAN ALSO BE REACHED BY SCHOONERS, MOST OF WHICH DEPART IN THE MORNING FROM THE CARENAGE, RETURNING THE FOLLOWING DAY. CHECK HOTEL FOR SAILING TIMES AND FARES.

CAR HIRE: A LARGE RANGE OF VEHICLES ARE AVAILABLE FOR HIRE FROM LOCAL AND INTERNATIONAL COMPANIES IN ST GEORGES OR ST ANDREW'S. CREDIT CARDS ARE NOT ALWAYS ACCEPTED BY HIRE COMPANIES. DRIVERS MUST BE OVER 21. MOST LOCAL AGENCIES HAVE SMALL FLEETS AND A MINIMUM THREE-DAY RENTAL PERIOD.

CRUISE LINER PASSENGERS: OVER 170 CRUISE SHIPS VISIT GRENADA DURING THE CRUISE SEASON RUNNING FROM OCTOBER TO APRIL. TOURS CAN BE BOOKED ON BOARD OR AT A CRUISE WELCOME CENTRE.

MELVILLE STREET TERMINAL: ON DISEMBARKING AT THE MELVILLE STREET CRUISE TERMINAL EXIT DIRECTLY THROUGH THE NEWLY OPENED ESPLANADE SHOPPING MALL AND OUT TO DOWNTOWN ST. GEORGE'S. THERE ARE EXCELLENT BUS AND TAXI FACILITIES FOR AN EFFICIENT TRANSFER OF PASSENGERS TO WAITING TOURS. THERE IS ALSO A DEDICATED WATER-TAXI JETTY FOR EASY TRANSFER OF PASSENGER TO WAITING WATER TAXIS.

INNER HARBOUR TERMINAL: IF DISEMBARKING AT THE INNER HARBOUR, EXIT ONTO THE PICTURESQUE CARENAGE WATERFRONT, WITH ITS TRADITIONAL ARCHITECTURE, SHOPS AND RESTAURANTS. THE CRUISE WELCOME CENTRE IS AT THE NORTH END OF THE QUAY.

GETTING AROUND:

GRENADA — CAR RENTAL CONTACT NUMBERS
ADAMS AUTO RENTALS, TEL: 444 3170
ARCHIE RENTALS, TEL: 439 0086
AZAR'S RENTAL, TEL: 414 2911
AVIS (SPICE ISLAND RENTALS), TEL: 440-3936
CHRIS & NICKY RENTAL, TEL: 443 2881
DABS CAR RENTAL, TEL: 444 4116
DAVID'S CAR RENTAL, TEL: 444-3399
DOLLAR RENT-A-CAR, TEL: 444-4786
FAS CAR RENTAL, TEL: 443 2293
GABRIEL'S RENTALS, TEL: 443 2304
GENERAL RENT A CAR, TEL: 440 2894
INDIGO CAR RENTALS, TEL: 439 3300
ISLAND RENT-A-CAR, TEL: 443-5624
J & B RENTALS, TEL: 435 5029
JERRY'S AUTO, TEL: 440-1730
MCINTYRE BROS. LTD. AUTO RENTALS, TEL: 444-3944
MAITLAND'S RENTALS, TEL: 444-4022
MCR CAR RENTALS, TEL: 440-2832
NED'S RENTAL, TEL: 440 5599
SANVIC'S 4X4 JEEP RENTALS, TEL: 444-4753
SUNSHINE TOURS, TEL: 444-2831

Getting Around:

Thomas & Sons, Tel: 444-4384

Thrift, Tel: 444-4984

Y&R Car Rentals, Tel: 444-4448

Carriacou — Car rental contact numbers

Martin Bullen, Tel: 443-7204

John Gabriel, Tel: 443-7454

Tour Operators:

A & E Tours, Tel: 435 1444

Adventure Jeep Tour, Tel: 444 5337

Barefoot Holidays, Tel: 444-4519

Carib Tours, Tel: 444-4363

Caribbean Horizon Tours, Tel: 444-3944

Dave Tours, Tel: 444 1596

Dopco Tours, Tel: 444 4732

Grenada Tours & Travel, Tel: 440-2031

Henry's SafariTours, Tel: 444-5313

Insight Tourism, Tel: 444 3697

Kennedy's Tours, Tel: 444 1074

K & J Tours, Tel: 440-4227

Mandoo Tours, Tel: 407 0024

Otway Tours, Tel: 440 2558

Pete's Mistique Tours, Tel: 440 1671

Spiceland Tours, Tel: 440-5127

Sunsation Tours, Tel: 444-1594

Telfor Walking Tours, Tel: 442-6200

Buses:

St. George's to: Annandale EC$2.50, Concorde EC$3, Grand Anse EC$2, Grand Etang EC$3.50, Grenville EC$5.50, Gouyave EC$4, La Sagesse EC$3, Sauteurs EC$6, Victoria EC$4.50, Westerhall EC$2.50.

What to do when you arrive!

Weddings: Grenada, Carriacou and Petite Martinique are pretty and relatively unspoilt and provide the perfect setting for a wedding. No blood or medical tests are required. Many hotels offer wedding packages and independent wedding planning services.

Legal Requirements: Three days minimum residency in Grenada, including weekends and public holidays. On the third day an application for a Marriage Licence must be made in person at the Office of the Prime Minister where you also pay the necessary stamp duty and licence fees. Generally the licence is ready within two working days. It may take longer if either partner is divorced as the application has to go to the Ministry of Legal Affairs for approval.

Documentation Required:

- Valid Passports
- Birth Certificates
- Sworn Affidavit (or letter from a Clergy Man, Lawyer or Registry), attesting that neither party has been married previously
- Decree Absolute, for each divorced party
- If widowed, the deceased's Death Certificate
- Legal proof if a name was changed by Deed Poll
- If under the age of 21, written parental consent by way of an Affidavit from a Lawyer or Notary Public.

All documents must be in English. If the originals are in another language, they must be translated into English and certified

Excursions and tours to places of interest:

Grenada offers good value activities to suit all budgets and activity levels. Tour options include - scuba diving, kayaking, biking, rainforests, waterfalls and tropical gardens, forts and plantations. An absolute must is a visit to the Spice Estate and Rum Distillery Tours. Grenada has six parishes - St George, St David, St Andrew, St Mark, St Patrick and St John — all with interesting sights and things to do.

St George's:

St George's, the capital city of Grenada is in the parish of St George. St George's is on the southwest coast near one of the island's best beaches, Grand Anse. Places of interest include:

The Carenage: a picturesque horseshoe shaped inner harbour with many18th-century warehouses, shops and restaurants. It is the entry point for visitors arriving by sea and provides a good introduction to Grenada.

The Esplanade: located on the bay side of St George's. Taxis and busses leave from here to all parts of the island.

Fort George: is the police's HQ It was built by the French in 1705 and is the oldest structure still standing in Grenada. It is worth a visit for the breathtaking views of the Carenage, harbour and coastline.

GRENADA NATIONAL MUSEUM: LOCATED ON THE SITE OF AN OLD ARMY BARRACKS AND PRISON BUILT IN 1704, THIS IS A SMALL BUT VERY INTERESTING MUSEUM JUST OFF YOUNG STREET, AND IS A GOOD STARTING POINT TO GET AN OVERALL SENSE OF THE ISLAND'S HISTORY.

QUEEN'S PARK: A NATIONAL PARK AND HOME TO THE NEW NATIONAL STADIUM IS USED FOR FOOTBALL, CRICKET AND ALL INTERNATIONAL SPORTS. THE FORMER STADIUM, SEVERELY DAMAGED BY HURRICANE IVAN IN 2004, HAS BEEN REPLACED BY A GBP £20 MILLION (US$40 MILLION) ULTRA MODERN SPORTING VENUE, FINANCED AND BUILT BY THE CHINA ANHUI FOREIGN CONSTRUCTION GROUP. THE NEW NATIONAL STADIUM, CAPACITY 16,061, HOSTED SIX OF THE CRICKET WORLD CUP SECOND STAGE SUPER 8 SERIES FROM 10 TO 20 APRIL 2007.

MARKET SQUARE: ESTABLISHED IN 1791, IS A BUSTLING, VIBRANT, COLOURFUL MARKET AND CENTRE OF LIFE FOR NOT ONLY GRENADIANS LIVING IN THE CAPITAL, BUT OF THE NATION.

AROUND GRENADA

ST ANDREW: ST ANDREW IS THE BREADBASKET PARISH. IT IS THE PARISH WITH THE LONGEST COASTLINE AND THE LARGEST PRODUCER OF THE ISLAND'S MAIN AGRICULTURAL EXPORTS. IT IS HOME TO THE OLD TOWN OF GRENVILLE, NAMED LA BAYE BY THE FRENCH; IT IS AFFECTIONATELY KNOWN AS RAINBOW CITY. PLACES OF INTEREST:

GRAND ETANG NATIONAL PARK & FOREST RESERVE: POPULAR FOR HIKING AND TREKKING. INSIDE THE FOREST GRAND ETANG LAKE, IS A NATURAL WATER FILLED CRATER OF ONE OF GRENADA'S EXTINCT VOLCANOES. A VISIT TO THIS SITE IS AN ABSOLUTE MUST FOR ANYONE WITH A PASSION FOR TROPICAL BIRDS, FLOWERS, RARE ORCHIDS AND WATERFALL.

GRENVILLE NUTMEG PROCESSING STATION: ONE OF THE LARGEST NUTMEG PROCESSING FACTORIES ON THE ISLAND

SHRINE OF OUR LADY OF FATIMA: THE DIOCESAN SHRINE OF OUR LADY OF FATIMA IS AT BATTLE HILL. REBUILT IN 1996 IT IS A PLACE OF GREAT SPIRITUAL INTEREST. THERE ARE AT LEAST NINE PILGRIMAGES A YEAR FROM THE OLD ROMAN CATHOLIC CHURCH IN GRENVILLE TO THE SHRINE.

ST PATRICK: THE MOST NORTHERLY OF PARISHES, WHICH STILL HAS MANY BEAUTIFUL OLD COLONIAL HOMES AND ESTATES HOUSES, SOME STILL WITH ALL THEIR ORIGINAL FEATURES. THE PRINCIPAL TOWN, SAUTEURS, IS NAMED AFTER A REAL HISTORICAL EVENT IN THE MID-17TH CENTURY WHEN THE NATIVE CARIBS LEAPT TO THEIR DEATH INSTEAD OF SURRENDERING TO THE FRENCH. PLACES OF INTEREST:

LEVERA NATIONAL PARK: THE 450-ACRE PARK HAS A STRONG REPUTATION AS GRENADA'S MOST SCENIC AND SPECTACULAR COASTAL AREA. FIRST STOP SHOULD BE THE LEVERA CENTRE — WHICH PROVIDES INFORMATION ABOUT THE PARK, GUIDES AND WHERE IT IS SAFE TO SWIM.

RIVER ANTOINE RUM DISTILLERY: THIS PRIVATELY OWNED DISTILLERY IS THE OLDEST FUNCTIONING WATER PROPELLED-DISTILLERY IN THE CARIBBEAN. SOME RUM MAKING PRACTICES ARE STILL IN USE THAT HAVE NOT CHANGED SINCE THE 1800. GUIDED TOURS ARE AVAILABLE.

LAKE ANTOINE: A SHALLOW CRATER LAKE WHICH IS HOST TO A VARIETY OF WILDLIFE. THE LAKE'S PERIMETER PROVIDES FOR A BEAUTIFUL WALKING TRAIL, WHILE THE LAKE AND SURROUNDING AREA IS AN EXCELLENT BIRD WATCHING SITE.

ST JOHN: THE HOME OF GOUYAVE, 'THE TOWN THAT NEVER SLEEPS'. THE HIGHLIGHTS OF THE PARISH ARE FISH FRIDAY FESTIVAL AND THE ANNUAL CELEBRATION OF THE FISHERMAN'S BIRTHDAY.

DOUGLASTON SPICE ESTATE: A MONUMENT TO GRENADA'S PAST AND A CHANCE TO SEE WHERE MOST OF THE SPICES ARE GROWN AND INITIALLY PROCESSED.

GOUYAVE NUTMEG PROCESSING STATION: ONE OF THE LARGEST NUTMEG PROCESSING FACTORIES ON THE ISLAND.

ST DAVID: ST DAVID GROWS TRADITIONAL CROPS OF COCOA, SPICES AND SUGAR CANE. PLACES TO VISIT:

WATERHALL RUM DISTILLERY: LOCATED ON THE WESTERHALL ESTATE, THE DISTILLERY CONTAINS SOME OF THE OLD ARTEFACTS AND EQUIPMENT THAT WERE USED IN THE REFINERY PROCESS.

LA SAGESSE NATURE CENTRE: LOCATED IN AN ESTUARY ALONG THE SOUTH-WESTERN COAST THIS IS ONE OF THE BEST BIRD WATCHING LOCATIONS ON THE ISLAND. ALSO HAS THREE BEACHES WITH SUPERB CORAL REEFS NEARBY

LAURA'S HERB & SPICE GARDEN: LOCATED NEAR PERDMONTEMPS, THESE GARDENS CONTAIN SAMPLES OF ALL THE ISLANDS HERBS AND SPICES

MT HARTMAN DOVE SANCTUARY: LOCATED NEAR WOBURN BAY, HOME TO THE PROTECTED GRENADA DOVE.

© *ADVENTURE JEEP TOURS*

CARRIACOU: CARRIACOU HAS SUPERB BEACHES, OLD-STYLE RUM SHOPS, EXCELLENT DIVING AND AMAZING SCENERY. THE NAME COMES FROM THE CARIB WORD FOR THE 'LAND OF REEFS', AND WITH ITS SIX-MILE BARRIER REEF ON THE EASTERN SIDE OF THE ISLAND, THE REASON FOR THE NAME IS CLEAR. CARRIACOU IS ALSO HOME TO 'KICK 'EM JENNY, A STILL ACTIVE UNDERWATER VOLCANO. PLACES OF INTEREST

BELAIR NATIONAL PARK (BELAIR): INCLUDES THE RUINS OF FRENCH AND ENGLISH OCCUPATION AND AN OLD SUGAR WINDMILL.

HIGH NORTH PEAK: AT 955FT, THIS IS THE HIGHEST ELEVATION ON THE ISLAND. THE AREA IS A PROTECTED NATIONAL PARK. TOUR GUIDES ARE AVAILABLE.

TYRREL BAY: A NATURE TRAIL FROM TYRREL BAY, PLUS A SHORT BOAT RIDE, WILL TAKE YOU INTO THE MIDDLE OF ONE OF THE MOST PRISTINE ECOSYSTEMS IN THE REGION, WHERE YOU CAN OBSERVE OYSTERS IN THEIR NATURAL HABITAT.

SANDY ISLAND MARINE PARK (HILLSBOROUGH): WITH ITS CLEAR BLUE WATERS AND STUNNING CORAL REEFS, THIS IS AN IDEAL LOCATION FOR SNORKELLING AND DIVING.

WHITE ISLAND MARINE PARK (WHITE ISLAND): BEAUTIFUL, ISOLATED WITH SHOALS OF EXOTIC TROPICAL FISH, IDEAL FOR SNORKELLING FOLLOWING BY PICNIC IN AN IDYLLIC SETTING

ANGLICAN RECTORY GARDENS: FORMERLY AND OLD BEAUSEJOUR GREAT HOUSE, THIS SITE IS STEEPED IN HISTORY AND ALSO HAS AN AMAZING CACTUS COLLECTION.

CARRIACOU BOTANICAL GARDENS (HILLSBOROUGH): TYPICAL BOTANICAL GARDEN WITH A WIDE VARIETY OF TROPICAL PLANTS, FLOWERS AND TREES.

GUN POINT (PETIT CARENAGE): NAMED AFTER THE CANNON ERECTED BY THE BRITISH IN THE 1780S.

THE CARRIACOU MUSEUM: LOCATED IN PATERSON STREET IN A RESTORED COTTON GIN MILL AND MANAGED BY THE CARRIACOU HISTORICAL SOCIETY. THE MUSEUM HAS A COLLECTION OF AMERINDIAN ARTEFACTS AS WELL AS EXHIBITS TRACING THE EARLY FRENCH, BRITISH AND AFRICAN SETTLEMENT.

CANUTE CALLISTE ART GALLERY: THE BEST GALLERY FOR LOCAL FOLK-ART PAINTING.

WATERFALLS:
GRENADA: ANNANDALE FALLS - LOCATED ON THE OUTSKIRTS OF ST GEORGE'S AND ARE EASILY ACCESSIBLE FROM THE CAPITAL.

CONCORD FALLS: LOCATED IN THE CONCORD VALLEY, ST JOHN, IS ACTUALLY THREE PICTURESQUE WATERFALLS. THE FIRST STAGE IS ACCESSIBLE FROM THE ROAD AND IS IDEAL FOR SWIMMING. THE SECOND STAGE AU COIN AND THIRD STAGE FOUNTAINBLEU ARE ONLY ACCESSIBLE ON FOOT. AT FOUNTAINBLEU, THE WATER CASCADES DOWN A 65-FOOT CLIFF INTO THE CRYSTAL CLEAR POOL BELOW.

HONEYMOON FALLS: (ST ANDREW): AT THE BASE OF MT QUA QUA.

ROYAL MT CARMEL FALLS (ST ANDREW): ALSO KNOWN AS THE MARQUIS FALLS, ARE THE HIGHEST ON THE ISLAND, CASCADING OVER 70FT. THESE FALLS ARE ACCESSIBLE BY FOOT. THERE IS AN ENTRANCE FEE, CURRENTLY US$1.00

ROSEMOUNT FALLS : ARE PRIVATELY OWNED AND ONLY ACCESSIBLE TO PEOPLE LUNCHING AT THE ROSEMOUNT PLANTATION HOUSE IN ST JOHNS.

SEVEN SISTERS FALLS (ST ANDREW): LOCATED CLOSE TO GRAND ETANG FOREST RESERVE. ACCESSIBLE ON FOOT AFTER A HALF HOUR WALK THROUGH THE FOREST. IT IS RECOMMENDED TO USE A GUIDE AS THE FALLS ARE ON PRIVATE PROPERTY,

VICTORIA FALLS: LOCATED AT THE FOOTHILLS OF MOUNT ST CATHERINE IN ST MARKS, ACCESSIBLE ON FOOT.

EATING OUT

IN GRENADA, FLAVOURS FROM DIFFERENT CULTURES COMBINE TO PRODUCE A UNIQUE CUISINE THAT IS DISTINCTLY GRENADIAN. CREOLE CUISINE AND SEAFOOD ARE THE ISLAND'S SPECIALTIES AND THE INSPIRATION FOR SOME OF THE BEST RESTAURANTS. AND, OF COURSE, ALL GRENADIAN CUISINE IS ENHANCED BY THE WIDE VARIETY OF LOCALLY GROWN SPICES, INCLUDING NUTMEG, CINNAMON, VANILLA, AND GINGER.

SEAFOOD OF ALL KINDS IS VERY POPULAR AND PLENTIFUL. LOCAL SPECIALTIES INCLUDE GRENADIAN CAVIAR (ROE OF WHITE SEA URCHIN), CONCHES (LAMBI) AND A FISH DISH CALLED "STUFFED JACKS" APPEARING ON MANY RESTAURANT MENUS. OTHER POPULAR DISHES INCLUDE CALALOO SOUP, CRABS, AND NUTMEG ICE-CREAM. BUT, NONE CAN BEAT THE TASTE OF "OILDOWN," GRENADA'S NATIONAL DISH. THIS IS A STEW, BUT A STEW AS YOU HAVE NEVER TASTED BEFORE, MADE WITH SALTED MEAT, BREADFRUIT, ONION, CARROT, CELERY, DASHEEN AND DUMPLINGS, ALL SLOWLY STEAMED IN COCONUT MILK UNTIL THE LIQUID IS ABSORBED. DIVINE!

MOST HOTELS AND RESTAURANTS OFFER INTERNATIONAL CUISINE, SERVING A VARIETY OF ENGLISH, FRENCH, ITALIAN AND AMERICAN DISHES. MOST PEOPLE DRINK THE LOCAL RUM OR CARIB BEER. BARS ARE STOCKED WITH WELL-KNOWN BRANDS OF WINES, WHISKY, RUM AND BRANDY.

GRENADA
ALOE VERA RESTAURANT: TEL: 405 8888

AQUARIUM RESTAURANT: POINT SALINES BEACH; TEL. 444-1410. OPEN DAILY, EXCEPT MONDAY, 10AM-11PM. WEDNESDAY NIGHT SPECIALS AND SUNDAY BEACH BBQ.

BANANAS RESTAURANT: TEL: 444 4662

B's Crab Back: Tel: 435 7058

Beach Side Terrace: The Flamboyant Hotel, Grand Anse Beach; Tel. 444-4247 Open daily, 7:30am-10:30pm. Major credit cards accepted. Sunday Beach BBQ with calypso and reggae music; entertainment most nights. International and local cuisine.

Blue Orchid Hotel & Restaurant: Grand Anse; Tel. 444-0999. Family Night specials on Thursdays and Saturdays. American, local and seafood dishes. No alcoholic beverages sold, but you can bring your own.

Carib Sushi: Tel: 439 5640

Choo Light Restaurant & Bar: L'anse aux Epines; Tel. 444-2196. Open Mon. to Sat. 11am-3pm and 6pm-11pm; Sun. and holidays 5pm-11pm. Indoor/outdoor garden setting. Specialties: Chinese Stir-fry and steamed seafood, chicken, and fish.

Coconut's Beach Restaurant: Grand Anse Beach; Tel. 444-4644. Open daily, except Tue. 12noon-10pm. Reservations advised. BBQ and live music Wed., Fri., and Sun. in season. Specialties: Local lobster, French Creole cuisine.

Creole Shack: Tel: 435 7422

De Big Fish: Tel: 439 4401

Deyna's: Melville Street, St. George's; Tel. 440-6795. Open daily, 7:30am-10pm, serving breakfast, lunch and dinner; waterfront view. Authentic Grenadian home cooking and refreshing local drinks, like Lime Squash.

Dodgy Dock Restaurant: Tel: 443 8783

Dr. Grooms Cafe & Restaurant: Point Salines; Tel. 444-1979. Italian and West Indian cuisine.

Ebony Restaurant: Victoria Street, Grenville. Open Mon. to Sat. 6:30pm-11pm and Sun. 10:30am-6pm. Crab and Calallo, lobster, sea eggs, spicy jerk pork, and classic fish steaks.

Fish and Chick Restaurant & Bar: Sugar Mill Roundabout, Grand Anse; Tel. 444-4132 Open daily, 7am until late; take-out service available. Fish, Chicken and Hot Roti, with daily West Indian specials.

Fox Inn Restaurant: Point Salines; Tel. 444-4123. West Indian and International cuisine.

Gath's Restaurant: Tel: 439 3408

Green Flash: Siesta Hotel, Grand Anse; Tel. 444-4645/6. Open daily, 8am-11am and 6pm-9:30pm; poolside dining. Specialties: Breakfast (daily specials, homemade muffins, fruit, and coffee); dinner (steak, lobster, and specialties du jour such as enchilada, moussaka, and fresh seafood). No alcoholic beverages sold, but you can bring your own.

Indigo's: True Blue Inn; Tel. 444-2000. A cool, relaxed setting overlooking the bay. Specialties: Seafood dishes.

Judith's Eating Delights: Gore Street; Tel. 440-5732. Open Mon. to Sat., 8:30am-6.00pm; Fri. 8am-8pm. Specialties: Refreshing local drinks, tasty fish and chicken snacks, and authentic local dishes.

Kentucky Fried Chicken: Granby Street & Grand Anse, St. George's; Tel. 440-3821

Kudos Bar & Grill: Tel: 444 1250

La Belle Creole: Blue Horizon Garden Resort, Grand Anse; Tel. 444-4316. Specialties: West Indian and Continental cuisine.

La Boulangerie Restaurant: Tel: 444 1131

La Chateau Restaurant: Tel: 444 2552

La Luna Restaurant: Tel: 439 0001

La Sagesse Restaurant: La Sagesse Nature Center; Tel. 444-6458. Open for lunch, dinner, and snacks. Specialties: Seafood, with a local and Continental menu.

Mi Hacienda Restaurant: Tel: 439 2799

Mona Lisa Restaurant: Tel: 439 6555

Morne Fendue Plantation Great House: Sauteurs; Tel. 442-9330. West Indian cuisine. Nick's Donut World - Le Marquis Complex, Grand Anse. Open Mon. to Sat. 7:30am-7:30pm; Sun. 9:30am-1pm and 4pm-7:30pm. Donuts and coffees.

Nutmeg: The Carenage, St. George's; Tel: 440-2539. Specialties: West Indian cuisine.

Oliver's Restaurant: Tel: 444 4258
Pirate's Cove Restaurant & Bar - Grand View Inn, Morne Rouge, Grand Anse; Tel: 444-2342. Open daily, 5pm for cocktails; 7pm-10:30pm for dinner. Bar open late with special menu and music. International and French cuisine.

RHODES RESTAURANT: TEL: 444 4334

THE RED CRAB: L'ANSE AUX EPINES; TEL: 444-4424. SPECIALTIES: WEST INDIAN AND INTERNATIONAL CUISINE.

GRENADIAN BY REX RESORTS: POINT SALINES, ST. GEORGE'S; TEL: 444-3333. INTERNATIONAL AND CARIBBEAN CUISINE SERVED IN FOUR RESTAURANTS. SPECIALTIES: SPECIAL BUSINESS LUNCH AND DINNER IN THE INTERNATIONAL RESTAURANT; DINNER IN THE ORIENTAL RESTAURANT; BARBECUES ON THE CARIBBEAN TERRACE; NIGHTLY ENTERTAINMENT.

RICK'S CAFÉ: GRAND ANSE SHOPPING CENTRE; TEL: 444-4597. OPEN DAILY, EXCEPT MONDAY SPECIALTIES: PIZZA, NUMEROUS FLAVOURS OF ICE CREAM, HAMBURGERS, BBQ RIBS, BAKED POTATOES, AND MORE.

ROCK'S INN RESTAURANT & BAR: H.A. BLAZE STREET, ST. GEORGE'S HARBOUR; TEL: 440-0088

ROYDON'S GUEST HOUSE: GRAND ANSE, ST. GEORGE'S; TEL: 444-4476. OPEN DAILY FOR BREAKFAST AND DINNER. RESERVATIONS RECOMMENDED. LOCAL FOOD IN A CHARMING ATMOSPHERE.

SAPPHIRE RESTAURANT: TEL: 439 3900

SUR LA MER RESTAURANT & AQUARIUS BEACH PAVILION: GEM HOLIDAY RESORT, MARNE ROUGE; TEL: 444-4224/1189. OPEN DAILY. BREATHTAKING SUNSET VIEW WHILE DINING ON THE BEACHFRONT.

TERRACE RESTAURANT: CROWNE PLAZA RESORT; TEL. 444-4371. MUSIC AND NIGHTLY ENTERTAINMENT. SPECIALTIES: WEST INDIAN AND INTERNATIONAL CUISINE.

TRAFFIC LIGHT BAR & GRILL: BELMONT, ST. GEORGE'S; TEL: 440-3375. WEST INDIAN CUISINE.

TROPICANA: LAGOON ROAD, ST. GEORGE'S; TEL: 440-1586. OPEN DAILY, 7:30AM-MIDNIGHT; TAKE-OUT SERVICE AVAILABLE. SPECIALTIES: LOCAL AND CHINESE CUISINE.

TURNING POINT DINER: TEL: 439 5186

WATER'S EDGE RESTAURANT: TEL: 443 2822

CARRIACOU

CALLALOO RESTAURANT & BAR: HILLSBOROUGH; TEL: 443-8004. WEST INDIAN AND INTERNATIONAL CUISINE.

CARIBBEE INN: PROSPECT; TEL: 443-7380. CANDLELIGHT DINNERS IN CHARMING OLD WORLD SURROUNDINGS, WITH SPECTACULAR VIEWS. SPECIALTIES: FRENCH CREOLE HOME COOKING.

POIVRE ET SEL: TYRREL BAY; TEL: 443-8390. FRENCH CUISINE.

ROOF GARDENS: HILLSBOROUGH; TEL: 443-7204. WEST INDIAN CUISINE.

SCRAPER'S: TYRREL BAY; TEL: 443-7403. SEAFOOD DISHES.

WHAT'S THE SCOOP/GRAMMA'S BAKERY: TEL: 443-7256. ICE CREAM AND BAKED GOODS.

SHOPPING:

SHOPPING HOURS: MON-FRI 0800-1600, SAT 0800-1300. SUPERMARKETS ARE USUALLY OPEN MON-SAT 0900-1900. FROM EXOTIC SPICES, LEATHER CRAFT, JEWELLERY TO STRAW GOODS PRINTED COTTONS AND OTHER HANDICRAFTS; GRENADA HAS SOMETHING THAT WILL APPEAL TO EVERYONE REGARDLESS OF AGE, GENDER OR SIZE OF POCKET! ST. GEORGE'S MARKET IS THE CENTRE OF CAPITAL'S SHOPPING. BUT THERE ARE A NUMBER OF SOUVENIR, GIFT AND HANDICRAFT SHOPS ESPECIALLY ON YOUNG STREET AND THE CARENAGE. THE BEST BUYS IN GRENADA ARE BATIK AND SCREEN PRINTED TEXTILES, LOCALLY MADE HANDICRAFT, LEATHER CRAFT, AND WOOD CARVINGS.

THE GRAND ANSE SHOPPING CENTRE AND LE MARQUIS COMPLEX OFFER SHOPS, CLOTHING STORES, RESTAURANTS AND ART GALLERIES. THE NEW SPICELAND MALL ALSO HAS A WIDE VARIETY OF SHOPS AND BOUTIQUES. ATTRACTIVE JEWELLERY IS SOLD BY SPICE ISLAND JEWELLERY. SPICES, LOCALLY MADE JAMS, JELLIES, AND SYRUPS, ESPECIALLY NUTMEG, LOCAL FRESH FRUITS AND VEGETABLES ARE OTHER GOOD BUYS. GRENADA HAS SOME NOTABLE LOCAL RUMS AND LIQUEURS THAT WILL MAKE SUPERB GIFTS AND WILL BE IDEAL FOR THE BBQ'S BACK HOME.

ON DISEMBARKING AT THE MELVILLE STREET CRUISE TERMINAL ENTER THE NEWLY OPENED ESPLANADE SHOPPING MALL AND ACCESS A SHOPPING EXPERIENCE IN PICTURESQUE, DOWNTOWN ST. GEORGE'S.

GRENADA ALSO OFFERS GOOD DUTY-FREE BARGAINS. MOST OF THE DUTY FREE SHOPS ARE LOCATED ON THE CARENAGE IN ST. GEORGE'S OR AT POINT SALINES INTERNATIONAL AIRPORT, INCLUDING GITTENS DUTY FREE SHOPS FOR PERFUMES AND COSMETICS; BON VOYAGE FOR JEWELLERY, CRYSTAL, AND OTHER GIFTS; COLOMBIAN EMERALDS FOR A FINE SELECTION OF QUALITY JEWELLERY, LAND FOR LEATHER GOODS AND DUTY FREE CARIBBEAN FOR GIFTS, SOUVENIRS AND DUTY FREE RUMS AND SPIRITS.

NIGHTLIFE:

HOME TO THE VIBRANT CALYPSO AND REGGAE MUSIC, GRENADA OFFERS A GOOD MIX OF LOCAL AND INTERNATIONAL RESTAURANTS AND BARS. MANY RESORTS PROVIDE NIGHTTIME ENTERTAINMENT, SUCH AS DISCOS, ORGANIZED SHOWS AND CABARETS. THE RENO CINEMA HAS RECENTLY BEEN REFURBISHED AND HOSTS MANY MULTI-CULTURAL EVENTS AS WELL AS SHOWING MOVIES.

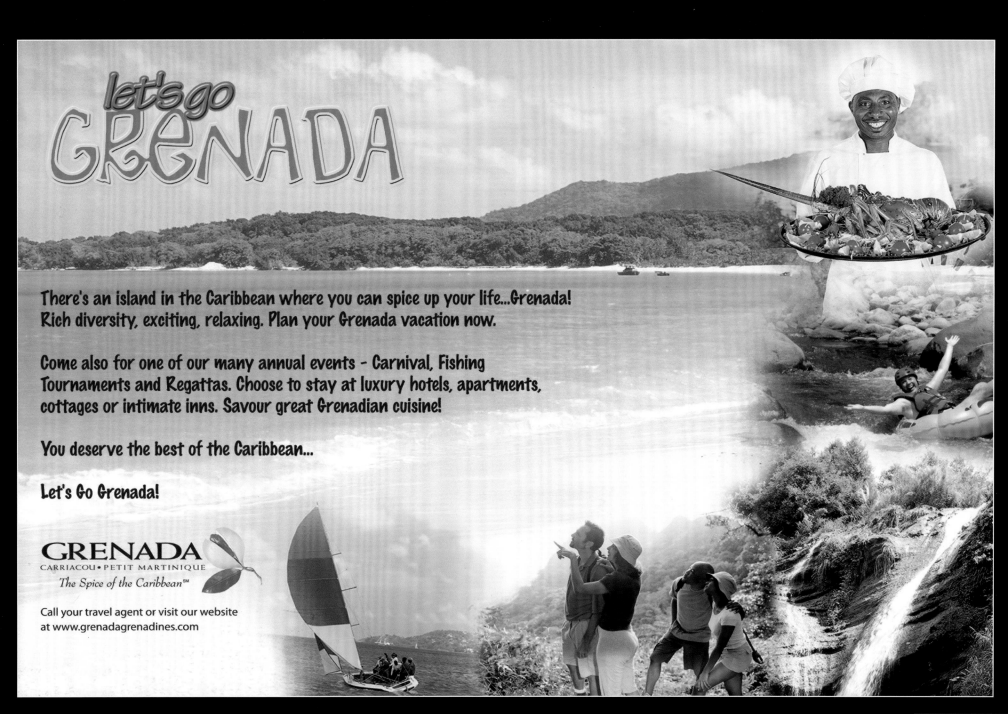

CLUB BANANAS: TEL: 444 4662. LOCATED IN TRUE BLUE, OPEN 10:30PM UNTIL LATE. THURS — LATIN; FRI - CARIBBEAN NIGHT AND SAT - INTERNATIONAL NIGHT.

LA SIRENA BEACH BAR: TEL: 444 1410. LIVE REGGAE ON SUNDAYS AND FEATURED NIGHTS. OPEN 10.00 AM - 12.00 MIDNIGHT (CLOSED ON MONDAYS).

THE DODGY DOCK BAR RESTAURANT & LOUNGE BAR: TEL: 443 8783. OPEN DAILY UNTIL MIDNIGHT.

THE OWL SPORTSBAR: TEL: 444 4247. HOME OF GRENADA'S LONGEST HAPPY HOUR! OPEN DAILY FROM 4PM FOR SNACKS, SPORTS TV, POOL, COCKTAILS, PARTIES & RELAXATION

SPORTS
THE GRENADA GOLF AND COUNTRY CLUB: IS A 9-HOLE COURSE NEAR TO GRAND ANSE AND OPEN TO VISITORS. EQUIPMENT IS AVAILABLE TO HIRE. TEL: 473 444 4128

TENNIS: THERE ARE PUBLIC COURTS AT GRAND ANSE, BUT MOST HOTELS HAVE THEIR OWN FACILITIES OR WILL MAKE ARRANGEMENTS.

HEALTH & FITNESS CLUBS & SPAS
JANISSA'S SPA: SPICE ISLAND BEACH HOTEL. FREE FOR GUESTS
CITRUS PARADISI: CALABASH HOTEL
AMANDA MARGA YOGA CENTRE: ST GEORGE'S TEL: 444 5880
THE BODY SHOP: GRAND ANSE, TEL: 444 4290
CARRIACOU FITNESS CLUB: HILLISBOROUGH, TEL: 443 8439
ISLAND MAGIC MASSAGE CLINIC: GRENADA RENAISSANCE HOTEL, TEL: 444 3306
SHAMAR: ST GEORGE'S, TEL: 440 6880

WATERSPORTS
GRENADA'S BEST-KNOWN WHITE-SAND BEACH IS THE GRAND ANSE. BUT THERE ARE SEVERAL OTHER GOOD BEACHES, NOTABLY THOSE ON NEIGHBOURING MORNE ROUGE, THE DESERTED BEACHES ON THE SOUTHERN COAST AND LEVERA BAY, WHICH IS ALSO A FAVOURITE SURFING SPOT.

TURTLE WATCHING: GRENADA IS HOME TO FOUR OF THE WORLD'S SEVEN VARIETIES OF TURTLES: THE SMALL ENDANGERED HAWKSBILL (ERETMOCHELYS IMBRICATA), THE LARGE NESTING LEATHERBACK (DERMOCHELYS CORIACEA) THAT CAN REACH UP TO 7FT, THE MIGRATORY LOGGERHEAD (CARETTA CARETTA) AND THE GREEN (CHELONIA MYDAS). FROM MARCH-JULY YOU CAN TAKE A MOONLIGHT TOUR TO LEVERA NATIONAL PARK TO WATCH LEATHERBACK TURTLES BURY THEIR EGGS IN THE SAND. REMEMBER A PRODUCT MADE FROM TURTLE SHELL IS ILLEGAL.

DOLPHIN AND WHALE WATCHING: ABOUT 15 SPECIES OF WHALE PASS GRENADA AND IN THE SEASON BETWEEN DECEMBER AND APRIL THERE IS A GOOD CHANCE OF SEEING THEM. OCCASIONALLY DOLPHINS JOIN IN THE FUN AND DANCE AT THE BOW OF YOUR YACHT AS YOU CRUISE ALONG. WITH A 95% SUCCESS RATE OF SEEING A WHALE OR DOLPHIN, THIS IS A GREAT DAY OUT FOR ALL THE FAMILY.

DEEP-SEA FISHING: THE ANNUAL SPICE ISLAND GAME FISHING TOURNAMENT ATTRACTS PROFESSIONALS FROM ALL OVER THE WORLD. BUT EVEN IF YOU ARE NOT A PRO, THERE ARE CHARTER COMPANIES THAT OFFER DAY TRIPS TO THE SAME FISHING GROUNDS. BEST TIME IS FROM NOVEMBER TO MARCH WHEN YOU HAVE A GOOD CHANCE OF CATCHING BOTH BLUE AND WHITE MARLIN, YELLOWFIN TUNA, WAHOO, SAILFISH, AND MORE. MOST OF THE BIGGER HOTELS CAN ARRANGE FISHING TRIPS. FOR INFORMATION ABOUT THE ANNUAL GAME FISHING TOURNAMENT, CONTACT ROBERT MILLER ON 473 444 2220.

SCUBA DIVING AND SNORKELING: GRENADA HAS A NUMBER OF EXCELLENT AS YET UNEXPLORED SNORKELLING AND DIVE LOCATIONS. THE LONG OFFSHORE REEF ON THE WEST OF THE ISLAND IS MARKED BY THE 600-FOOT WRECK OF THE BIANCA C, A CRUISE LINER THAT CAUGHT FIRE IN THE HARBOUR AND SANK AS IT WAS BEING TOWED AWAY IN 1961. THERE IS A SMALL MONUMENT IN THE CARENAGE GIFTED BY THE ITALIAN GOVERNMENT TO THE PEOPLE OF GRENADA FOR THEIR BRAVERY IN SAVING THE LIVES OF THE PASSENGERS TRAPPED ON THE BIANCA C.

THE MOST CONVENIENT SNORKELLING IS FOUND IN THE AREA JUST SOUTH OF GRAND ANSE BEACH. MOST DIVE SITES ARE EASILY ACCESSIBLE FROM THE COAST. SOME OF THE BEST ARE MOLINIÈRE REEF, LOCATED APPROXIMATELY 5KM (3 MILES) FROM ST GEORGE'S; MARTIN'S BAY, CLOSE TO GRAND ANSE, ALSO A POPULAR SNORKELING SPOT; AND CHANNEL REEF. BUT, FOR THE REAL ADVENTUROUS DIVER THE BEST DIVING IS AROUND CARRIACOU. ALTHOUGH LARGELY UNDEVELOPED, CARRIACOU IS ACCESSIBLE BY BOAT AND PLANE, OFFERS A NUMBER OF ACCOMMODATIONS, AND IS ENCIRCLED BY MARVELLOUS, PRISTINE REEFS.

DIVE SHOPS - GRENADA
AQUANAUTS: TEL: 444 1126 (TRUE BLUE) OR TEL: 439 2500 (GRAND ANSE). GRENADA'S PREMIER DIVE CENTER WITH 2 LOCATIONS, BEST DIVE BOATS & EQUIPMENT, SHOPPING, NITRO, OFFERS FREE TRANSFERS FROM HOTELS & DEDICATED SNORKEL TRIPS.
DEVOTION2OCEAN: TEL: 444 3483
DIVE GRENADA: TEL: 444 1092
ECO DIVE: TEL: 444 7777
SCUBA TECH GRENADA: TEL: 439 4346

DIVE SHOPS: CARRIACOU
ARAWAK DIVERS: TEL: 443 6906
CARRIACOU SILVER DIVING: TEL: 443 7882
LUMBA DIVE: TEL: 443 8566

© MARLIN FISHING TRIP ON 'YES AYE.COM'

YACHTING: GRENADA AND ITS SISTER ISLANDS OF CARRIACOU AND PETITE MARTINIQUE ARE KNOWN FOR THEIR SPECTACULAR CLEAR WATERS. LOCATED OUTSIDE OF THE HURRICANE BELT AT 12° N, THE ISLANDS PROVIDE SMOOTH SAILING AND SAFE ANCHORAGE, ALL YEAR ROUND. CARRIACOU, THE GATEWAY TO THE GRENADINES, IS THE PERFECT STARTING POINT FOR A SAILING VACATION UP THE ISLANDS, AND THERE ARE COMPANIES WHO WILL ARRANGE BARE BOATS, CREWED YACHTS OR CHARTERS TO SUIT YOUR VACATION NEEDS.

GRENADINES, IS THE PERFECT STARTING POINT FOR A SAILING VACATION UP THE ISLANDS, AND THERE ARE MANY COMPANIES WHO WILL ARRANGE BARE BOATS, CREWED YACHTS OR CHARTERS TO SUIT YOUR VACATION NEEDS.

GRENADA AND CARRIACOU ARE EXTREMELY POPULAR WITH A NUMBER OF MAJOR YACHT RACES AND REGATTAS HELD THROUGHOUT THE YEAR, NOTABLY THE JANUARY SAILING FESTIVAL (LASTING FIVE DAYS) AND THE SAILING REGATTA IN TYRELL BAY ON CARRIACOU. POPULAR SAILING DESTINATIONS INCLUDE THE GRENADINE ISLANDS SUGAR LOAF, GREEN ISLAND AND SANDY ISLAND. A VARIETY OF LARGE AND SMALL CRAFT ARE AVAILABLE FOR HIRE:

CARIB'S CATS: TEL: 444 3222
CLUB MARINER WATERSPORTS: TEL: 444-4439
FOOTLOOSE YACHT CHARTERS: TEL: 440 7949
HORIZONS YACHT CHARTERS: TEL: 439 1000
ISLAND YACHT CHARTERS: TEL: 443 5624
MARTIN'S MARINA: TEL: 444 4439
SPICE ISLAND MARINE SERVICES: TEL: 444-4257
FIRST IMPRESSIONS: TEL: 440-3678

TRADITIONAL SCHOONERS:

VISITORS CAN ALSO MAKE BOAT TRIPS ON TRADITIONAL WOODEN SCHOONERS, WHICH IS A POPULAR WAY TO CROSS THE 5KM- (3-MILE) DISTANCE BETWEEN THE ISLANDS OF CARRIACOU AND PETIT MARTINIQUE. FARE IS $EC20 SINGLE, $EC30 RETURN. TRIP TAKES 3-4 HOURS. FERRY SERVICE SCHEDULE:THE CARENAGE, GRENADA, TO CARRIACOU: TUES 9:30AM; WED 10:00AM; FRI 11:00AM; SAT 8:00AM; SUN 7:00AM. HILLSBOROUGH, CARRIACOU, TO GRENADA: MON 10:00AM; WED 9:30AM; THUR 10:00AM; SAT 9:00AM; SUN 5:00PM.

ISLAND HOPPING:

GRENADA IS IDEALLY SITUATED FOR ISLAND HOPPING. THERE ARE FERRY LINKS ALONG THE GRENADINES FROM GRENADA TO ST VINCENT. THE FIRST STOP SHOULD BE CARRIACOU, WHICH IS SMALL, JUST EIGHT MILES BY FIVE MILES, AND STILL LARGELY UNDEVELOPED. HIGH SPEED FERRIES TAKE JUST OVER AN HOUR FROM GRENADA. ALSO IDEAL FOR A DAY TRIP ON A SAILING BOAT.

CONTINUE NORTH OF CARRIACOU TO THE GRENADINES ANY OF WHICH IS AN IDYLLIC ALTERNATIVE. CHOOSE FROM THE DELIGHTFUL BEQUIA, SOPHISTICATED MUSTIQUE, TINY MAYREAU OR ANY ONE OF THE PRIVATE ISLANDS SUCH AS PALM ISLAND OR PETIT ST VINCENT. IF YOU ARE STAYING ON THE SOUTHWEST OF GRENADA THE RAINFOREST RETREAT AROUND SOUFRIERE IN ST LUCIA IS AN ATTRACTIVE OPTION.

FINALLY, IF YOU SIMPLY WANT TO INJECT SOME PACE INTO YOUR HOLIDAY YOU COULD TAKE A SHORT-BREAK FROM GRENADA TO ONE OF THE OTHER ISLANDS. SIMPLY CATCH AN INTER-ISLAND FLIGHT TO NEARBY BARBADOS, TOBAGO AND ST VINCENT OR FURTHER A FIELD TO JAMAICA AND PUERTO RICO.

WALKING: THE GRAND ETANG NATIONAL PARK AND FOREST RESERVE CONTAINS NUMEROUS MARKED TRAILS. THE ROAD TO THE PARK PASSES BY THE NORTHWESTERN EDGE OF MOUNT SINAI.

ACCOMMODATION

HOTELS: GRENADA OFFERS A VARIETY OF MODERN, LUXURIOUS HOTELS. PRE-BOOKING IS ESSENTIAL. AN 8 PER CENT GOVERNMENT TAX IS ADDED TO ALL HOTEL AND RESTAURANT BILLS, AND A 10 PER CENT SERVICE CHARGE (SUBJECT TO CHANGE WITH INTRODUCTION OF VAT) IS ADDED TO THE BILL BY MANY HOTELS AND RESTAURANTS. THERE ARE SEVERAL GUESTHOUSES, SOME OF WHICH OFFER SELF-CATERING FACILITIES AND A GROWING NUMBER OF PRIVATELY OWNED APARTMENTS AND VILLAS AVAILABLE FOR HIRE. CONTACT THE GRENADA BOARD OF TOURISM FOR UP TO DATE DETAILS.

CAMPING: CAMPING IS NOT ENCOURAGED BECAUSE THERE ARE NO PROPER CAMPING FACILITIES. HOWEVER, IT IS POSSIBLE TO CAMP IN CERTAIN PLACES BUT ONLY WITH THE PRIOR PERMISSION OF THE LANDOWNER.

WHERE TO STAY IN GRENADA, CARRIACOU & PETITE MARTINIQUE:

GRENADA HOTELS:

ALLAMANDA BEACH RESORT & SPA: GRAND ANSE, ST GEORGE'S. TEL:(473) 444-0095
EMAIL: SIESTA@SPICEISLE.COM

BEL AIR PLANTATION RESORT: CORINTH, ST DAVID. TEL: 444 6305
EMAIL: BELAIR@SPICEISLE.COM

BLUE HORIZONS COTTAGE HOTEL: MORNE ROUGE, ST. GEORGE'S. TEL: (473) 444-4316
EMAIL: BLUE@SPICEISLE.COM

BLUE ORCHID HOTEL & RESTAURANT: GRAND ANSE, ST. GEORGE'S. TEL: (473) 444-0999
EMAIL: DOVETAIL@SPICEISLE.COM

CALABASH HOTEL, L'ANSE AUX EPINES: ST. GEORGE'S. TEL: (473) 444-4334
EMAIL: CALABASH@SPICEISLE.COM

CINNAMON HILL RESORT & BEACH CLUB: GRAND ANSE, ST. GEORGE'S. TEL: (473) 444-4301
EMAIL: CINHIL@SPICEISLE.COM

COYABA BEACH RESORT: GRAND ANSE, ST. GEORGE'S. TEL: (473) 444-4129
EMAIL: COYABA@SPICEISLE.COM

'Model is wearing Yaki One Extensions'

Style in the Sun

Women in the Caribbean always want to look Hot Hot Hot!

Sleek offers everything under the sun to do with hair. Whether you're looking to add volume, length, highlights or lowlights, Sleek has all the products you could possibly want.

Sleek can transform your hair into a vision of loveliness, whether you're into sultry curls, kinky fros or just looking for the ultimate Sleek straight look.

To see our comprehensive collection of extension hair, wigs, braids and accessories in a fabulous range of colours visit us online.

Alternatively, if you would like to distribute Sleek products in the Caribbean, call our sales hotline on +44 (0) 208 988 5502

www.sleek.co.uk

○ Siesta Hotel

Useful Information

FLAMBOYANT HOTEL: GRAND ANSE, ST. GEORGE'S. TEL: (473) 444-4247
EMAIL: FLAMBO@SPICEISLE.COM

GEM HOLIDAY BEACH RESORT: MORNE ROUGE BAY, ST. GEORGE'S. TEL: (473) 444-3737
EMAIL: GEM@SPICEISLE.COM

GRENADA CROWNE PLAZA RESORT: TEL: 444 4371

POINT SALINES HOTEL: TEL: 444 4123

REX GRENADIAN, POINT SALINES: ST. GEORGE'S. TEL: (473) 444-3333
EMAIL: GRENREX@SPICEISLE.COM

RIVERA HOTEL: GRAND ANSE, ST. GEORGE'S. TEL/FAX: (473) 444-4537

SIESTA HOTEL: MORNE ROUGE, ST. GEORGE'S. TEL: (473) 444-4646
EMAIL: SIESTA@SPICEISLE.COM

SPICE ISLAND BEACH RESORT: GRAND ANSE, ST. GEORGE'S. TEL: (473) 444-4258
EMAIL: SPICEISL@SPICEISLE.COM

TRUE BLUE INN: TRUE BLUE, ST. GEORGE'S. TEL: (473) 443-2000
EMAIL: TRUEBLUE@SPICEISLE.COM
VICTORIA HOTEL, QUEEN STREET, VICTORIA, ST. MARK'S. TEL: (473) 444-9367

GUEST HOUSES

ALMOST PARADISE GUEST HOUSE: TEL: 442 0608
BAILEY'S INN: SPRINGS, ST. GEORGE'S. TEL: (473) 440-2912
BARRY'S COUNTRY RETREAT: TEL: 442 0330
BEECH INN: TEL: 444 4216
CABIER OCEAN LODGE: TEL: 444 6013
EPPING FOREST GUEST HOUSE: TEL: 440 3333
GRENADA RAINBOW INN: GRAND BRAS, ST. ANDREW'S. TEL: (473) 442-7714
HOMESTEAD GUEST HOUSE: GOUYAVE, ST. JOHN'S. TEL: (473) 444-8526
HUMMINGBIRD INN: GRAND ANSE, ST. GEORGE'S. TEL/FAX: (473) 444-4216
JENNY'S PLACE: TEL: 439 5186
LA SAGESSE NATURE CENTRE: ST DAVID'S. TEL/FAX: (473) 444-6458
EMAIL: LSNATURE@SPICEISLE.COM
MITCHELL'S GUEST HOUSE: BLAIZE STREET, ST. GEORGE'S. TEL: (473) 440-2803
ROCKS INN: BLAIZE STREET, ST. GEORGE'S. TEL: (473) 440-0088

ROYDON'S GUEST HOUSE: GRAND, ST. GEORGE'S. TEL/FAX: (473) 444-4476
SAM'S INN: DUNFERMLINE, ST. ANDREW'S. TEL: (473)-442-7313
ST. ANN'S GUEST HOUSE: PADDOCK, ST. GEORGE'S.TEL: (473) 440-2717
SIMEON'S INN: GREEN STREET, ST. GEORGE'S. TEL: (473) 440-2537
SUNSET VIEW BEACH HOUSE: TEL: 440 5758
TOWN & COUNTRY GUEST HOUSE: TEL: 444 4516
TROPICANA INN, LAGOON ROAD: ST. GEORGE'S. TEL: (473) 440-1586
WINDWARD SANDS INN: GRAND ANSE, ST. GEORGE'S. TEL/FAX: (473) 444-4238
YACHT'S VIEW: LAGOON ROAD, ST. GEORGE'S. TEL: (473) 440-3607

APARTMENTS

CORAL COVE COTTAGES & APARTMENTS: L'ANSE AUX EPINES, ST. GEORGE'S.
TEL: (473) 444-4422. EMAIL: CORALCV@SPICEISLE.COM

GRAND VIEW INN: MORNE ROUGE, ST. GEORGE'S. TEL: (473) 444-4984
EMAIL: GVINN@SPICEISLE.COM

HIDEAWAY APARTMENTS: GRAND ANSE, ST. GEORGE'S. TEL/FAX: (473) 444-0011
KIKI APARTMENTS, TEL: 439 5137

LANCE AUX EPINES COTTAGES: L'ANSE AUX EPINES, ST. GEORGE'S. TEL: (473) 444-4565
EMAIL: COTTAGES@SPICEISLE.COM

LAZY LAGOON: TEL: 443 5209

LEXUS INN: BELMONT, ST. GEORGE'S. TEL: (473) 444-4780

PALM COURT APARTMENTS: GRAND ANSE, ST. GEORGE'S. TEL: (473) 444-4453

PETIT BACAYE COTTAGE HOTEL: WESTERHALL, ST. GEORGE'S. TEL/FAX: (473) 443-2902

R.S.R. APARTMENTS: LAGOON ROAD, ST. GEORGE'S. TEL: (473) 440-3381

SOUTH WINDS HOLIDAY COTTAGES & APARTMENTS: GRAND ANSE, ST. GEORGE'S.
TEL: (473) 444-4310. EMAIL: CDAVID@SPICEISLE.COM

THOMAS & SONS APARTMENTS: TEL: 444 4384

TWELVE DEGREES NORTH: L'ANSE AUX EPINES, ST. GEORGE'S. TEL: (473) 444-4580
EMAIL: 12DEGRSN@SPICEISLE.COM

VILLAS OF GRENADA: TEL: (473) 444-1896. EMAIL: gpm&vog@Spiceisle.com

WAVE CREST HOLIDAY APARTMENTS: GRAND ANSE, ST. GEORGE'S. TEL/FAX: (473) 444-4116

CARRIACOU

ADE'S DREAM GUEST HOUSE: HILLSBOROUGH. CARRIACOU. TEL: (473) 443-7317
EMAIL: adesdea@Spiceisle.com

ALEXIS LUXURY APARTMENTS: TYRELL BAY, CARRIACOU TEL/FAX: (473) 443-7179

BAYALEAU POINT COTTAGES: WINWARD, CARRIACOU. TEL/FAX: (473) 443-7984
EMAIL: goldhill@Spiceisle.com

BOGLES ROUND HOUSE COTTAGES: BOGLES, CARRIACOU. TEL/FAX: (473) 443-7841
EMAIL: goldhill@Spiceisle.com

CARRIACOU YACHT & BEACH CLUB: TYRELL BAY, CARRIACOU. TEL: (473) 443-6123

CARIBBEE INN: PROSPECT, CARRIACOU. TEL: (473) 443-7380
EMAIL: caribbee@caconnet.com

DOWN ISLAND VILLA RENTALS: CRAIGSTON, CARRIACOU. TEL: (473) 443-8182
EMAIL: uskabder@Spiceisle.com

GRAMMA'S LUXURY APARTMENTS: HILLSBOROUGH, CARRIACOU. TEL: (473) 443-7255
HOPE'S INN, L'ESTERRE, CARRIACOU. TEL: (473) 443-7457

MILLIE'S GUEST HOUSE: HILLSBOROUGH, CARRIACOU. TEL: (473) 443-7310

MOM & DAD HOLIDAY APARTMENTS: BELMONT, CARRIACOU. TEL: (473) 443-8056

PARADISE INN: L'ESTERRE VILLAGE CARRIACOU. TEL: (473) 443-8406
EMAIL: paradise@caconnet.com

PATTY'S VILLA: HILLSBOROUGH CARRIACOU. TEL: (473) 443-8412

PEACE HAVEN GUEST HOUSE: HILLSBOROUGH, CARRIACOU. TEL: (473) 443-7475

SCRAPER'S HOLIDAY COTTAGES: TYRELL BAY, CARRIACOU. TEL: (473) 443-7403

SEASIDE FOUNTAIN GUEST HOUSE: HARVEY VALE, CARRIACOU. TEL: (473) 443-7425

SILVER BEACH RESORT: HILLSBOROUGH, CARRIACOU. TEL: (473) 443-7337
EMAIL: silverbeach@grenadines.net

THE SAND GUEST HOUSE: HILLSBOROUGH, CARRIACOU. TEL: (473) 443-7100

PETITE MARTINIQUE

MIRACLE MART GUEST HOUSE, PETITE MARTINIQUE. TEL: (473) 443-9065
SEASIDE VIEW HOLIDAY COTTAGES, PETITE MARTINIQUE. TEL: (473) 443-9007

CALENDAR: FEBRUARY – JANUARY

GRENADA HAS A NUMBER OF FESTIVALS, YACHTING AND FISHING EVENTS THROUGHOUT THE YEAR, IN ADDITION, PUBLIC HOLIDAYS. DATES FOR THESE EVENTS ARE SUBJECT TO CHANGE. IT IS ADVISED TO CONTACT THE GRENADA BOARD OF TOURISM FOR FULL DETAILS OF EVENTS.

GRENADA CARNIVAL (AUGUST)

THE ANNUAL CARNIVAL IS ONE OF THE ISLAND'S BIGGEST FESTIVALS WITH THE MAIN ACTIVITIES IN ST. GEORGE'S. THE FESTIVITIES BEGIN IN JULY WITH THE OPENING OF CALYPSO TENTS, HOTS UP IN EARLY AUGUST WITH CALYPSO SHOWS ALMOST EVERY NIGHT OF THE WEEK. FINAL COUNTDOWN TO CARNIVAL BEGINS ONE WEEK BEFORE, WITH THE OPENING OF THE RAINBOW CITY FESTIVAL, ALSO CALLED LA BAYE, IN GRENVILLE, ST ANDREW.

THE NATIONAL CARNIVAL SOCA MONARCH FINALS AND PANORAMA STEEL BAND COMPETITION ALL TAKE PLACE IN CARNIVAL WEEK ENDING ON CARNIVAL SUNDAY WITH THE DIMARCHE GRAS SHOW, FEATURING THE KINGS AND QUEENS OF THE FANCY MAS BANDS IN COMPETITION FOR KING AND QUEEN OF CARNIVAL. MANY GRENADIANS START AT THE DIMARCHE GRAS SHOW AND CONTINUE THROUGH J'OURVERT, WHERE IN THE EARLY HOURS OF MONDAY MORNING, THE TRADITIONAL JAB-JAB OR DEVIL MAS BANDS EMERGE FROM THE DARKNESS BLACKENED WITH STALE MOLASSES, TAR, GREASE, CREOSOTE OR MUD, AND WEARING LITTLE MORE THAN THEIR HORNED HELMETS. CARNIVAL MONDAY ENDS WITH THE MONDAY NIGHT MAS' STREET JUMP-UP, WHICH CONTINUES INTO THE EARLY HOURS OF TUESDAY MORNING.

ON CARNIVAL TUESDAY, THE COSTUME 'MAS' BANDS PARADE THROUGH THE STREETS OF ST. GEORGE'S, TO THE MUSIC OF TRADITIONAL STEEL BANDS OR THE PULSATING SOUNDS OF THE CURRENT CALYPSO SONGS FROM MOBILE DJS. THE PARTY CAN CONTINUE LONG INTO THE NIGHT UNTIL THE MOST DEVOUT OF REVELLERS FINALLY STAGGER HOME.
VISIT: "HTTP://WWW.SPICEMASGRENADA.COM"

DRUM FESTIVAL (APRIL)

NORTHEASTERN GRENADA IS HOME TO THE TIVOLI DRUMMERS AND THE NATURAL BIRTHPLACE OF THE GRENADA DRUM FESTIVAL. FOUNDED IN 1995 WITH THE GOAL OF SPREADING THE DRUM CULTURE, THE TIVOLI DRUMMERS HAVE DEVELOPED A UNIQUE STYLE OF CHOREOGRAPHED DRUMMING THAT IS NOT SEEN ELSEWHERE. THE IDEA FOR THE ANNUAL DRUM FESTIVAL WAS BORN WHEN LIVINGSTON KRUMAH NELSON,

THE DIRECTOR OF THE TIVOLI DRUMMERS VISITED GUADELOUPE IN 2000 AND WITNESSED THE FESTIVAL OF THE DRUMS REFERRED TO AS GWOKA. THE FIRST DRUM FESTIVAL WAS HELD IN 2001. FOR INFORMATION CONTACT LIVINGSTON NELSON ON TEL: 473 442-8890; MOBILE: (473) 409-1057; EMAIL: DRUMKRUMAH@SPICEISLE.COM OR VISIT: WWW.SPICEISLE.COM/DRUMKRUMAH

CARRIACOU: MAROON MUSIC FESTIVAL

THE PAST, PRESENT AND FUTURE MEETS IN THE ANNUAL MAROON MUSIC FESTIVAL ON GRENADA'S SISTER ISLES OF CARRIACOU AND PETITE MARTINIQUE. DANCERS WHIRL AND SING IN THE LOCAL PATOIS TO THE PULSATING BEAT OF THE BIG DRUM; SONGS THAT RECALL THEIR HISTORY AND ANNOUNCE THEIR FUTURE ASPIRATIONS. THE BEATING OF THE DRUMS LIFTS THE HEART AND CURES THE SOUL, BECKONING ALL, TO JOIN THE RING AND SUCCUMB TO THE RHYTHMS. THE FESTIVAL FEATURES THE BIG DRUM NATION DANCE, STRING BAND MUSIC, SHAKESPEARE MAS, QUADRILLE AND AFRICAN DANCE, INTEGRATING WITH THE MORE MODERN SOUNDS OF CALYPSO, REGGAE, SOUL AND BLUES. CONTACT THE CARRIACOU MAROON FESTIVAL ON TEL: 473 443 6555 OR VISIT:
WWW.GRENADINES.NET/CARRIACOU/MAROONMUSICFESTIVAL.HTML

CALENDAR GUIDE FEBRUARY TO JANUARY:

FEBRUARY
- ANNIVERSARY OF GRENADA INDEPENDENCE
- CARRIACOU CARNIVAL

MARCH
- ST PATRICK'S DAY FESTIVAL

APRIL
- 5TH ANNUAL GRENADA ROUND THE ISLAND EASTER REGATTA
- GOOD FRIDAY
- EASTER SUNDAY (CHANGING DATE)
- ANNUAL CARRIACOU MAROON MUSIC FESTIVAL

MAY
- LABOUR DAY
- WHIT MONDAY

JUNE
- CORPUS CHRISTI
- FISHERMAN'S BIRTHDAY CELEBRATIONS AUGUST

AUGUST
- CARRIACOU REGATTA FESTIVAL
- EMANCIPATION DAY
- GRENADA CARNIVAL MONDAY
- GRENADA CARNIVAL TUESDAY

OCTOBER
- GRENADA CRICKET CLASSICS FESTIVAL
- THANKSGIVING DAY

NOVEMBER
- ANNUAL TTSA CARRIACOU SAILING SERIES

DECEMBER
- CARRIACOU PARANG FESTIVAL
- CHRISTMAS DAY
- ST STEPHENS/ BOXING DAY

JANUARY
- NEW YEARS DAY
- ANNUAL SPICEISLE BRITISH TOURNAMENT
- ANNUAL LA SOURCE GRENADA SAILING FESTIVAL

The high-quality commercial complex in the heart of the city...

Downtown St. George's, the picturesque and historical capital of Grenada now boasts the following:

- A dedicated Cruise Port Terminal
- A new Welcome Centre
- The ultra-modern Esplanade Mall
- The Bruce Street Commercial Complex
- A bustling Bus Terminus and a host of new private sector initiatives.

WE ARE THE PULSE OF THE CITY - THE HEARTBEAT OF THE NATION !

QUICK FIND NUMBERS

EMERGENCY

POLICE/ FIRE	911
AMBULANCE (ST GEORGE'S)	434
AMBULANCE (ST ANDREW)	724
AMBULANCE (CARRIACOU)	774
COASTGUARD	399

MEDICAL CARE

GITTEN'S DRUG MART & GITTEN'S PHARMACY. TEL: 444 4954 (GRAND ANSE); TEL: 440 2165 / 3940 (HALIFAX STREET, ST. GEORGE'S)

ST GEORGE'S GENERAL HOSPITAL	440 2050
PRINCESS ALICE, MIRABEAU	442 725
PRINCESS ROYAL, CARRIACOU	443 7400

ST AUGUSTINE'S MEDICAL SERVICES INC. (PRIVATE 24/7 EMERGENCY). TEL: 440 6173/6174/6175

TELEPHONE

DIRECTORY ENQUIRES	411
OPERATOR ASSISTANCE	0
DIALING OUT	+011
DIALING IN	1 473

LOST/STOLEN CREDIT CARDS

AMERICAN EXPRESS	336/393 – 1111 (CALL COLLECT)
MASTERCARD	800-1561
VISA	410/902-8022 (CALL COLLECT)

LOST/STOLEN TRAVELERS CHEQUE

AMERICAN EXPRESS	800/452 0761

WESTERN UNION MONEY TRANSFER

RENWICK THOMPSON & CO- TEL: 439-5364 (ST GEORGE'S); TEL: 442-8353 (ST ANDREW'S); TEL: 437-0047 (ST JOHN); TEL: 442-0492 (ST PATRICK'S)
VENA BULLEN & SONS; TEL: 443-6471 (CARRIACOU)

TOURIST INFORMATION

GRENADA

GRENADA BOARD OF TOURISM

PO BOX 293, BURNS POINT, ST GEORGES, GRENADA. TEL: 440 2001 OR 440 2279.
FAX: 440 6637. E-MAIL: GBT@SPICEISLE.COM
WEBSITE: WWW.GRENADAGRENADINES.COM
GRENADA TOURISM OFFICE: 439 UNIVERSITY AVENUE TORONTO, ONTARIO M5G 1Y8 TEL: 416-595 1343

GRENADA TOURISM OFFICE: 439 UNIVERSITY AVENUE. TORONTO, ONTARIO M5G 1Y8.
TEL: 416-595 1343.

GRENADA TOURISM OFFICE: 11 BLADES COURT, 121 DEODAR ROAD, LONDON SW55 2NU.
TEL: 020-8877 4516.

GRENADA TOURISM OFFICE: 820 SECOND AVENUE, SUITE 900D, NEW YORK, NY 10017.
TEL: 212-687 9554.

GRENADA TOURISM OFFICE: P.O. BOX 1668, LAKE WORTH, FLORIDA, 33460 USA.
TEL: 561 588 8176.

GRENADA HOTEL ASSOCIATION: OCEAN HOUSE, P.O. BOX 440, MORNE ROUGE, ST GEORGES.
TEL: 444 1353; FAX: 444 4847
EMAIL: GRENHOTA@SPICEISLE.COM
WEBSITE: WWW.GRENADAHOTELSINFO.COM

BANKS

BANK OF NOVA SCOTIA: HALIFAX STREET, ST GEORGE'S
TEL: 473 440 3274

FIRST CARIBBEAN BANK: HALIFAX STREET, ST GEORGE'S
TEL: 473 440 3232

GRENADA CO-OPERATIVE BANK: CHURCH ST, ST GEORGE'S
TEL: 473 440 2111

REPUBLIC BANK (GRENADA) LTD OF GRENADA: CNR HALIFAX & HILLSBOROUGH STREET, ST GEORGE'S
TEL: 473 444 2265

RBTT GRENADA LTD: CORNER OF CROSS & HALIFAX STREET, ST GEORGE'S
TEL: 473 440 3521

FOREIGN EMBASSIES

BRITISH HIGH COMMISSION: NETHERLANDS BUILDING, GRAND ANSE, ST GEORGE'S TEL: 473-440-3222
E-MAIL: BHCGRENADA@SPICEISLE.COM

CONSULATE OF GERMANY: P.O. BOX 814, FORT JEUDY, NEW WESTERHALL POINT, ST. GEORGE'S, GRENADA
TEL: 473-443-2156

CONSULATE OF POLAND: C/O RENWICK & THOMPSON, THE CARENAGE, ST. GEORGE'S, GRENADA
TEL: 473-444-2274

Useful Information

CONSULATE OF SWEDEN: C/O TODAYS WONDERS, GRENVILLE STREET, ST. GEORGE'S, GRENADA
TEL: 473-440-2765

CONSULATE OF SPAIN: C/O JONAS BROWNE & HUBBARDS (G'DA) LTD., THE CARENAGE, ST. GEORGE'S, GRENADA. TEL: 473-440-2087

CONSULATE OF THE NETHERLANDS: ST. MARTIN'S, LUCAS STREET, ST. GEORGE'S, GRENADA
TEL: 473-440-3459
E-MAIL: grantjo@spiceisle.com

CONSULATE OF FRANCE: P.O. BOX 857 LB 42, 5 LUCA STREET, ST. GEORGE'S, GRENADA
TEL: 473-440-6349

CONSULATE OF ITALY: P.O. BOX 1312, ST. GEORGE'S, GRENADA. TEL: 473-444-5676
E-MAIL: tesoro@Spiceisle.com

CONSULATE OF JAMAICA: P.O. BOX 439, ST. GEORGE'S, GRENADA. TEL: 473-440-2451
E-MAIL: rtscsuwi@Spiceisle.com

CONSULATE OF GUYANA:
C/O GEORGE F. HUGGINS & CO. LTD. GRAND ETANG ROAD, ST. GEORGE'S, GRENADA TEL: 473-440-2031

EMBASSY OF THE REPUBLIC OF CHINA: TEL: 473-440-3054
E-MAIL: recemgnd@Spiceisle.com

UNITED STATES EMBASSY: L'ANSE AUX ÉPINES STRETCH, GRAND ANSE, ST GEORGE'S
TEL: 473-444-1173
E-MAIL: usemb_gd@Spiceisle.com

EMBASSY OF VENEZUELA: P.O. BOX 201, UPPER LUCAS STREET, ST. GEORGE'S, GRENADA
TEL: 473-440-1721. E-MAIL: labfam@Spiceisle.com

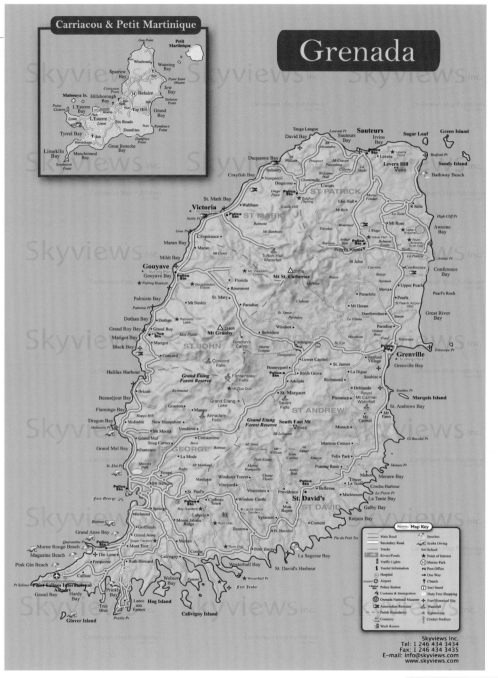

Grenada's Future Generations...

Grenada's famous son...

MIGHTY SPARROW

SLINGER FRANCISCO, KNOWN WORLDWIDE AS 'THE MIGHTY SPARROW' WAS BORN IN 1936 IN THE FISHING VILLAGE OF GRAN ROI, GRENADA. HE MIGRATED WITH HIS FAMILY TO TRINIDAD WHERE HIS VOCAL TALENT EMERGED AT A YOUNG AGE. HE BECAME HEAD CHOIRBOY OF ST PATRICK'S CATHOLIC CHURCH, SINGING BARITONE AND TENOR IN LATIN.

AT THE AGE OF 20, THE MIGHTY SPARROW BECAME RECOGNISED AS THE LEADING CALYPSONIAN WITH HIS RECORD-BREAKING HIT, 'JEAN AND DINAH' (1956), AND THROUGHOUT THE YEARS, HE SHOWCASED HIS VOCAL DIVERSITY WITH OVER 70 ALBUMS TO HIS CREDIT. HE WAS CROWNED CALYPSO MONARCH 11 TIMES AND WON THE ROAD MARCH TITLE 8 TIMES.

THIS ILLUSTRIOUS LYRICIST/COMPOSER/SINGER/COMEDIAN/ENTERTAINER IS APPRECIATED WORLDWIDE. IN ADDITION TO AN IMPRESSIVE ARRAY OF AWARDS THROUGHOUT HIS CAREER, HE RECENTLY RECEIVED THE SPECIAL ACHIEVEMENT AWARD FOR OUTSTANDING CONTRIBUTION TO GLOBAL MUSIC AT THE BOLLYWOOD 2006 MUSIC AWARDS. THE MIGHTY SPARROW IS THE UNRIVALED 'CALYPSO KING OF THE WORLD'.

Contributors...

A SPECIAL THANKS IS EXTENDED TO THE FOLLOWING PEOPLE FOR THEIR VALUABLE CONTRIBUTION TO THIS BOOK.

EDITOR & RESEARCHER - CANDY THOMPSON
DESIGNED BY - FRANK TYSON
CO-PRODUCTION & EDITING TEAM:
JOHN HUGHES
VALERY SMALL
PETER ADDISON
COLIN PILGRIM
EDWIN FRANK

PHOTOGRAPHY
ANGUS THOMPSON
MARIE FIELDEN
MAGDALENA FIELDEN
PAULINE SCOTT-GARRETT
CULLEN JOHN
JOHN CHARLES
PAUL GRAVEL
SUZANNE GAYWOOD
HAROLD QUASH
JOSHUA YETMAN
TUUL BATSAKHAU
GARY CLIFFORD
JULIA SNOW
RIA NARINE

SPORTS SHOTS
PA PHOTOS

UNDERWATER PHOTOGRAPHY
AQUANAUTS
CLAUS MEYER
RUSSELL HOUGH
JOHN DEVON
BRUCE DEVON
HARALD BOLTEN
PETER SEUPEL

SAILING SHOTS
OWNE VAN DER WAL

TOUR COMPANIES
FIRST IMPRESSIONS
ADVENTURE RIVER TUBING
ADVENTURE JEEP TOURS

SCHOOLS
BEACON SCHOOL
WESTMORLAND SCHOOL

FLORAL CONTRIBUTION
JOHN AND FAY MILLER